VAMPIRE
TAXONOMY

VAMPIRE TAXONOMY

[
IDENTIFYING AND INTERACTING
WITH THE MODERN-DAY BLOODSUCKER
]

MEREDITH WOERNER

A PERIGEE BOOK

A PERIGEE BOOK
Published by the Penguin Group
Penguin Group (USA) Inc.
375 Hudson Street, New York, New York 10014, USA
Penguin Group (Canada), 90 Eglinton Avenue East, Suite 700, Toronto, Ontario M4P 2Y3, Canada
(a division of Pearson Penguin Canada Inc.)
Penguin Books Ltd., 80 Strand, London WC2R 0RL, England
Penguin Group Ireland, 25 St. Stephen's Green, Dublin 2, Ireland (a division of Penguin Books Ltd.)
Penguin Group (Australia), 250 Camberwell Road, Camberwell, Victoria 3124, Australia
(a division of Pearson Australia Group Pty. Ltd.)
Penguin Books India Pvt. Ltd., 11 Community Centre, Panchsheel Park, New Delhi—110 017, India
Penguin Group (NZ), 67 Apollo Drive, Rosedale, North Shore 0632, New Zealand
(a division of Pearson New Zealand Ltd.)
Penguin Books (South Africa) (Pty.) Ltd., 24 Sturdee Avenue, Rosebank, Johannesburg 2196,
South Africa

Penguin Books Ltd., Registered Offices: 80 Strand, London WC2R 0RL, England

While the author has made every effort to provide accurate telephone numbers and Internet
addresses at the time of publication, neither the publisher nor the author assumes any responsibility
for errors, or for changes that occur after publication. Further, the publisher does not have any
control over and does not assume any responsibility for author or third-party websites or their
content.

First edition: November 2009

Library of Congress Cataloging-in-Publication Data

Woerner, Meredith.
   Vampire taxonomy : identifying and interacting with the modern-day bloodsucker /
Meredith Woerner.— 1st ed.
      p.   cm.
   Includes bibliographical references and index.
   ISBN 978-0-399-53579-6
   1. Vampires—Humor.   I. Title.
   PN6231.V27W64 2009
   814'.6—dc22   2009028619

PRINTED IN THE UNITED STATES OF AMERICA

10   9   8   7   6   5   4   3   2   1

Most Perigee books are available at special quantity discounts for bulk purchases for sales
promotions, premiums, fund-raising, or educational use. Special books, or book excerpts,
can also be created to fit specific needs. For details, write: Special Markets, Penguin Group (USA)
Inc., 375 Hudson Street, New York, New York 10014.

CONTENTS

INTRODUCTION

I am Dracula, and I bid you welcome . . .

—Count Dracula, Bram Stoker's *Dracula*

Take a deep breath. Everything you've been hoping, dreaming, or dreading is true: Vampires do indeed walk among us, no longer hidden in the shadows.

They attend our schools, sit on a stool next to us at our favorite pub, ride with us on the subway—they may even be our friends or neighbors.

So how does one deal with the day-to-day member of the undead?

With this guide, you'll begin your vampire education, learning how to decipher whether the person next door is a vampire, and if that vamp is friend or foe. *Vampire Taxonomy* was created in hopes of separating vampire truth from lies, to educate the masses on the rich history of pop vampirism.

WHY NOW?

Today, images of vampires confront us everywhere we look: Hordes of shrieking human fans wait in line to catch a glimpse of an actor pretending to be the immortal lover of their dreams, vampire kits are sold in bookstores, vampire-named bands climb the charts and fill our iPods, bite mark bandages sell in novelty stores, Twitter offers up vampire-centric backgrounds, there are vampire wines and energy drinks ("Vamp: for when the sun goes down"), Vlad D'Impaler has a Facebook page and operates Vampire.com from the comfort of his laptop in his coffin, and ancient undead lords in Muppet form teach our children how to count to five. Vampire society has literally infiltrated popular culture.

But it's not all hilarious puns and witty fang jokes. Real vampires do exist, and the rapid growth of vampire phenomena in popular culture is quiet but steady proof of the ever-expanding vampire race present in our world today. The more socially acceptable the vampire way becomes, the more it's likely that real vampires are leaking out actual nosferatu fact among our fiction.

Is this to say that all rumors about vampires are true? Heavens, no. But hopefully after thumbing through the pages of this book, you will finish with a well-rounded education on the vampires who live among you today.

No longer can we ignore the vampiric societal impact. It's only a matter of time before we reach the undead tipping point and vampire assimilation begins aggressively taking over our streets and towns. When this happens, you'll need to know exactly what works and what doesn't if you are to survive your day-to-day dealings with the undead.

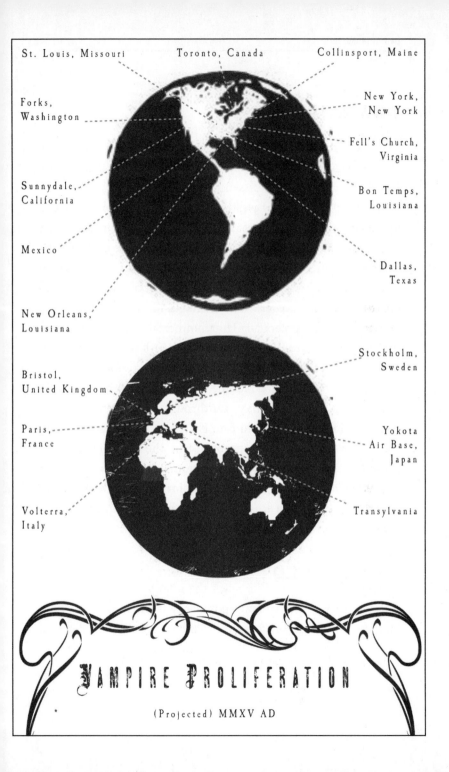

St. Louis, Missouri   Toronto, Canada   Collinsport, Maine

Forks,
Washington

New York,
New York

Fell's Church,
Virginia

Sunnydale,
California

Bon Temps,
Louisiana

Mexico

Dallas,
Texas

New Orleans,
Louisiana

Stockholm,
Sweden

Bristol,
United Kingdom

Paris,
France

Yokota
Air Base,
Japan

Volterra,
Italy

Transylvania

Vampire Proliferation

(Projected) MMXV AD

NOW WHAT?

This is where *Vampire Taxonomy* comes in. Consider this book a guide to sussing out what is real and what is fake in the vampire world.

In the following pages, we'll examine the vampire specimen and discuss its origins, physical makeup, and attitude.[1] After acquiring a general knowledge of the species, you'll learn how to deal with the fanged (or sometimes defanged) creature. Using evidence gleaned from a variety of media resources including books, films, TV, and otherwise, you'll discover the different classifications of vampires, how to identify a potentially lethal immortal from the annoying stalker love puppies, and how to assess the level of danger and proper human response to any vampire—friend or foe.

Finally, you'll receive real-life advice that can be used as a step-by-step guide to getting you through many common vampire situations. What should I do if my lab partner is a vampire who doesn't seem to have a problem with the way I smell? What should I do in the event of a vampire uprising? What's the proper etiquette when meeting a vampire's ex-lover? All of these important and practical concerns will be answered in Chapter 8.

WHY SHOULD I CARE?

As previously stated, vampire popularity is reaching an all-time high, but with this newfound celebrity and idolization comes a

---

1 Although both male and female vampires exist, for sake of ease, throughout this book, we've referred to general vampires as *he*, because most of the specimens discussed are indeed male.

misguided and unfounded sense of security. Pop culture vampires are becoming so wildly accepted and packaged that we're forgetting what the vampire mind really wants.

Blood.

They're after yours and your families' and loved ones', and just because we're living in a world that is embracing the undead doesn't mean one should sheepishly and blindly follow the trend. No, not all vampires are evil and hungry for the sweet blood of a virgin. But not all vampires are tragic loners looking for their one true love, either.

What we know for sure is that any and every vampire should be treated with caution. You can no longer turn a blind eye to the children of the night. Your life may be at stake.

1

THE COMPLETE VAMPIRE

I am neither good, nor bad, neither angel nor devil,
I am a man, I am a vampire.

—Michael Romkey, *I, Vampire*

Before discussing the various classifications of the vampire species, it is important to have a basic understanding of the typical specimen. Whether dealing with Romantic, Tragic, or Villainous Vampires, it will be helpful to know some general information about vampires in order to make an informed classification. This chapter will examine the many important features of the vampire, including the physical attributes of the fang and the great sparkle debate.

Although all attempts have been made here to present a general guideline for vampires, they're a constantly evolving and shifting species. We attempted to include all the general identifiers, history, and weaknesses of the most common vampires. But while you read this, somewhere out there a vampiric strain could very well be mutating to bring us a new bloodline of nosferatu with talents and traits we haven't seen before. It's a growing underground world shrouded in secrecy, so who knows what will await the supernatural world when the sun goes down?

WHERE DO VAMPIRES COME FROM?
VAMPIRE HERITAGE

The great mystery surrounding vampire creation has brought forth numerous tales of mystical lore. There are theories dating back to ancient folklore stating that children born with red hair and blue eyes were doomed to vampirism.[1] However, the hundreds of theories on vampire heritage don't help in finding a clear lineage from a first vampire Mother and Father to the leather-jacketed beasties you see roaming the streets today.

Will we ever know the original answer, as most vampires themselves hardly know who they are and where they came from? It's difficult to say. Most vampires in the know guard their secrets with fang and claw, so it may be a while until we have final confirmation on where this whole bloody mess began. But until then, it's at least good to have some theories.

The Mark of Cain and Lilith

One ancient theory as to how we got so many vampires running around is all thanks to the original first Earth lady—no, not Eve, but Lilith. According to ancient Jewish Apocrypha texts, Lilith was created first by God for the original man, Adam. Both Adam and Lilith were created from the Earth, and because they both came from the same place, Lilith refused to remain under Adam's thumb. When they couldn't see eye to eye, Lilith left Eden to start her own family (hence the next model human, Eve, was made from Adam's side, so she would always stay close).

God, not happy with the change in plans, sent a few angels to fetch

---

1 Noted in Heinrich Kramer and Jacob Sprenger's witchcraft guide *Malleus Maleficarum* ("The Hammer of [or Against] Witches"), published in 1487.

her back to Eden. Lilith made a deal with the angels so she could live on her own and in return became the mother of all demons.

Meanwhile Adam and Eve had their children Cain and Abel. As a young man Cain became jealous of his little brother and murdered him in a rage. Cain was then banished from his family's land and given a telltale "mark"; what exactly the mark constitutes is up for debate. As legend tells it, Cain stumbled into Lilith's territory, and the two hit it off. Their future children become the vampires we now know today.

Although there is no reference to Lilith in the Bible or the Torah (just in the Jewish Apocrypha texts that have yet to be confirmed and fall outside what the religion believes), Cain's unholy brood and a possible Lilith figure are referenced in *Beowulf*.[2]

Judas Iscariot

The other ancient theory popular among vampire creationists is the idea that vampires have all stemmed from the cursed former friend of Jesus, Judas Iscariot, the apostle who betrayed Christ and turned the Son of God over to the Romans. As folklore tells it, Judas, who ransomed Jesus for thirty silver pieces and then later committed suicide, was hexed. He and his entire family were cursed for their betrayal, and also for the suicide (which is considered a mortal sin). It does, however, lend some credence to the idea that silver is a vampire repellent.[3]

2 An interesting pop culture nod to the mother of all vampires is in the film *Tales from the Crypt Presents: Bordello of Blood*. Lilith herself is raised from the dead and can be controlled by one of the keys to the gate of Hell that's filled with the actual blood of Christ. Also it should be noted that the actress who played Lilith, Angie Everhart, is a redhead. Was that a direct nod to the (as legend would have it) ginger tresses of Judas or just a happy circumstance? The ancient mother was also given another nod in Marvel Comics' *Giant-Size Chillers*.

3 The film *Dracula 2000* took an interesting look into this creation legend. Gerard Butler, who played the evil vampire in the feature, is revealed in the end to be Judas Iscariot himself, living out his curse in modern times, doomed to walk the Earth

Vlad and Friends

Most vampire enthusiasts are aware that the historical figure Vlad III the Impaler, Prince of Wallachia, was more rumored than plausible as the Father of the vampiric species. The hype surrounding his surname, *Dracula* (Romanian for "son of the dragon"), is due to the success of Bram Stoker's work and the Dracula franchise. That being said, Vlad is a good example of the vampire heritage legend in which people in the past were punished for their unholy actions by being transformed into vampires. Vlad is infamously known as a brutal ruler and callous torturer. Rumor has it he was never stingy dealing out beheadings, burnings, boilings, skinnings, and, his favorite, impalings (hence his nickname). Eventually he was made to pay for his evil ways, though Dracula film lore would have you believe his transformation was all for love. It's easy to see how a historical savage could in legend get linked to an evil immortal being.

Other legends about humans so foul that they've turned vampire include rumored torturer and bloodbather Elizabeth Báthory and a small group of French knights from the Crusades. These unholy knights feasted on the flesh of their troops in order to stay alive while stranded in combat. This is where it gets a little blurry: Either the knights were promised immortal life by a demon or changed on their own because of their shameful cannibalism. Either way, they were left as vampires. Some legends have all of

---

forever. Judas has indeed been cursed with the mark of the vampire, never able to die for his ultimate betrayal. His character is not welcome in Heaven or Hell.

THE ORIGINAL TWILIGHT?

In 1887, an Irish author named Bram Stoker published *Dracula*. It wasn't a bestseller, but wasn't critically panned—in fact, it received a lot of praise. In 1899, it was published in America. From there it was translated into a play by Hamilton Deane (the man responsible for changing Drac from vile villain to gentleman), and eventually made its way to Broadway in 1927, featuring Béla Lugosi as the title character. The show ended up being Lugosi's springboard into cinema, where he donned the silken cape and genteel attitude.

But it was the 1922 German film *Nosferatu* that really got the hype machine started around Dracula. The unauthorized version of Stoker's *Dracula* was a silent film by Friedrich Wilhelm and starred Max Schreck as the infamous bulbous-headed Count Orlock. (It is also the film that singlehandedly popularized the concept that vampires could be killed with sunlight; even Dracula in the original novel can go out during the day.) The film kicked up a lot of legal dirt. Stoker's wife attacked the film for copyright infringement, and the case resulted in the ruling that all copies of *Nosferatu* be destroyed. However, prints had already been distributed around the world so it was nearly impossible to track them all down, which is why they exist today.

Stoker passed away in 1912, long before he could see the incredible highs that Dracula was destined to achieve all over the world, as well as the incredible number of changes his character would go through. He never lived to see Lugosi's gentle vampire take or watch Gary Oldman make Dracula a soppy romantic. Nor did he see the franchise grow into cartoons, comics, and cereals. Dracula was the first vampire sensation. And he never even had to sparkle.

the knights (except one sacrifice) leaving the war and starting vampire clans across the globe; others have one knight leaving on his own, soulless, ready to populate the world with vampires.[4]

PHYSICAL IDENTIFIERS

Now that you have a general idea of some of the vampire lore, it's time to learn how to spot 'em. Not all vampires are alike. Depending on the bloodline, different vamps will pick up different kinds of vampire traits. Eyes, appendages, and fangs are all passed on through the sire. This leads to a vast array of vampire characteristics.

Limbs

Vampires and their limbs usually fall under three different categories: those who sport unpleasant and scaly clawed hands all the time; those who over time have naturally evolved into having human-looking appendages; and those who can shape-shift between the human and beast look.

The immortal hand is a unique evolutionary feature on the vampire. As the public's attention has increasingly shifted onto vampires over the years, their physical appearance has needed to evolve. No longer can a lower-level vampire get by with deformed mitts similar to those of Max Schreck's Count Orlok, unless he has his own gang of lackeys to protect and shield him. Clawed hands with three-inch nails tend to bring unwanted attention down upon a vampire's head. So although you'll see the mutated

---

4 This was actually the foundation for the film *The Forsaken*, in which two Halfies do battle with one of the original knights, played by Johnathon Schaech.

talon hand of ancient times now and again, most vampires have evolved beyond the exposed claw.

Vampires brazen enough to flaunt the mangled unholy hand of the devil, so to speak, can usually be classified as Villains (see Chapter 3). Their overall appearance is generally unkempt, cadaverous, and quite frightening, and this extends to their seriously long and lethal fingers and nails. Their fingers appear twice the size of a normal digit, with long fingernails that can grow up to two or even three inches. These talonlike ends are razor sharp and when used with force can open up a neck with the mere wave of a hand. Generally these vampires do not spend a great amount of time interacting with humans—except to eat them—and so don't see any need to disguise their true form.

Also noteworthy is the power that vampire beasts have over their appendages. An outstretched vampiric arm can move well beyond a normal human's reach. Villains often use their Stretch Armstrong–like powers to sneak up on an unsuspecting victim. Ever feel a chilly hand on your back even though the closest person in the room is beyond your reach? Chances are it's the withered claw of a vampire about to caress your artery from behind. But you'll never catch him; he can move his body faster than your mere mortal eyes see.[5]

Because some species retain the ability to shape-shift, however, a remarkable number of vampires can transform between their less publicly acceptable appearance and their slightly more human shell easily and quickly. Not looking like a scaly-handed beast really helps with day-to-day dealings and even luring in prey.[6] It

---

5 Hence the media's attempt to re-create this ability in TV and on film with fast-forward and quick cuts.

6 Just ask stripper/snake-headed bloodsucker Santanico Pandemonium, as depicted in the film *From Dusk Till Dawn*.

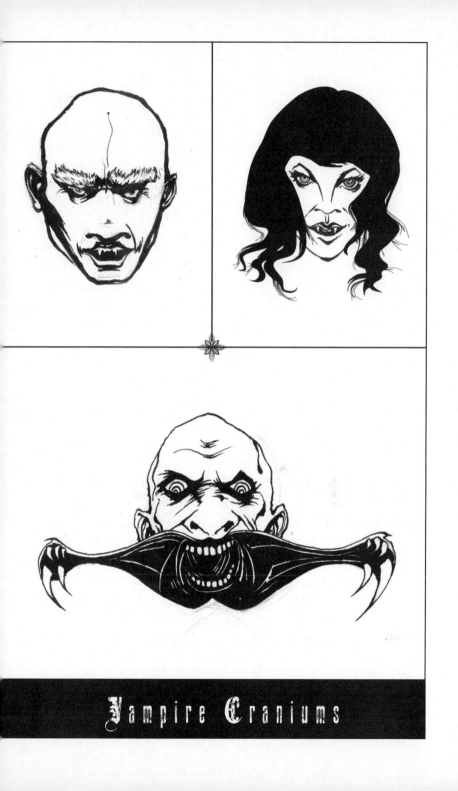

Vampire Craniums

is also a great benefit to vampires looking for love in the human world who may otherwise be shunned, particularly because their human appearance is usually quite pleasing. (And it has been reported that those longer-than-human fingers are quite an asset in the romance department.) But get the creature enraged, excited, or hungry and the claws will come out. And in the case of Villainous Vampires (see Chapter 3), they pack a deadly punch.

Many of the vamps who don't transform sport a scaled-back version of the lanky and mutated fist from centuries ago. Modern vamps have appendages that appear delicate but are in reality quite strong, all the way down to the tip of the sharp-as-a-knife fingernail. So be careful even around the fey vampires of late; they can still, most likely, throw you up against the wall, one delicate arm behind their back.

Eyes

More diverse than any other part of the vampire anatomy is the nosferatu eye. These blinking beauties come in all shapes and sizes, depending on the vampiric lineage or strain. Usually the maker's color and anatomy will be passed on to his vampire spawn.

Similar to a litmus test (or a mood ring), the eyes of a vampire can also tell you what the specimen is feeling; for example, if he's hungry, angry, or tired (all emotions to look out for when dealing with a vampire). The eye color change commonly reflects an increase in adrenaline, be it positive or negative. When you see a vampire eye flash, someone is excited—possibly in a very unhealthy (for you) way. There can also be a dietary-induced color change; the *Twilight* vampires, though they possess many questionable (even among vampires) and unique vampiric traits, have an interesting and sound reason for their optic irregularities.[7]

---

7 A recently turned vampire in the *Twilight* series, along with a vampire who has recently fed on human blood, will have crimson-hued eyes. A Twi-vamp's eyes

COMMON VAMPIRE EYE COLORS

ICE BLUE/WHITE/SILVER
Underworld
The Vampire Chronicles
Moonlight
Salem's Lot
Cold Hearts
Van Helsing
John Carpenter's Vampires

ONYX
Being Human
30 Days of Night
The Vampire Diaries
Blood Ties
The Dresden Files
Twilight series

**PALE YELLOW
(FEVER YELLOW)**
*The Lost Boys, Lost Boys:
     The Tribe*
Buffy the Vampire Slayer
     (TV series)
Blade
Salem's Lot ('70s miniseries)
Fright Night (1 and 2)
Vampire in Brooklyn

BLOOD RED
Bram Stoker's Dracula (movie)
Twilight series
Innocent Blood
Dracula 2000
Christopher Lee in almost all of
     his Dracula roles
Frostbiten

Often optic color changes are paired with a few other facial tics and features. You may see a Cro-Magnon-esque forehead grow to accompany the eye flash, or the mouth may increase in size. The *Buffy* series introduced the world to the not so easy to hide S.V.F., "Sexy Vampire Forehead."[8]

become jet black when his body needs blood, and the bruises under his eyelids (prominent because Twi-vamps don't sleep) become more pronounced when hungry. The Cullens have amber or gold-hued peepers because they feed specifically on animal blood.

8 Described by *Buffy's* Harmony on her vampire reality TV show in the *Buffy the Vampire Slayer* comic, Season 8, Issue 21, "Harmonic Divergence." The editors added a disclaimer,

Fangs

Similar to the eye, the vampire species has racked up quite the canine collection over the years. From the mangled overgrown incisors to the actual absence of a pointy-toothed grin, vampires and their fangs have been evolving since the first mention of that sharp smile in *Varney the Vampire: The Feast of Blood* in the 1840s. A great way to chart the evolutionary process of the vampiric race is hanging right from the mouths of the species.

It's no mistake that more and more vampires are popping up in the media and in pop culture without extended canines. The lack of fangs allows the creatures to blend in. If you look back over the years, the further back you go, the more exotic the teeth become. Think of the first set of movie fangs from *Nosferatu*. They were large and placed in front of the vampire's mouth, great for getting your lips over the puncture marks and sucking to your heart's desire, but terrible for speaking. Plus who's going to look at those chompers and *not* suspect that this person is a child of the night? The slow and steady reduction of the fang is a great representation of vampiric evolution.

Remember, the presence or absence of fangs is not enough information alone to classify a vampire. Nosferatu bites with both sharpened canines and dull teeth into the sweetest of victims. So do not think for a second that an absence of fang means you're safe.

Retractable Fangs

The most common set of fangs among the vampire community is the retractable canine. The teeth actually grow out of the vampire's gum line when the vamp is excited, angry, or hungry. Of course,

---

as they were guessing what Harm really meant when she said, "Tousled hair over the S.V.F. Exotic (the editors give us a note that they THINK it means 'Sexy Vampire Forehead')." This forehead is also used in *The Lost Boys, Lost Boys: The Tribe, Subspecies, Tales from the Crypt Presents: Bordello of Blood*, and *From Dusk Till Dawn*, to name a few.

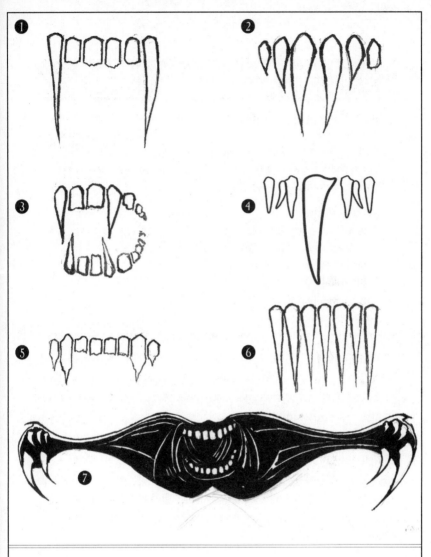

1. The classic overextended rattler or retractable fang set.

2. An earlier form of the front fang; you can imagine the difficulty the owner would have conversing.

3. The double fang, with a bottom set, highly decorative and unnecessary, but intimidating nonetheless.

4. The mangled mouth: not aesthetically appealing, but useful for intimidation.

5. Classic double fang, common among the retractable mouthed vampires.

6. Dagger jaw: this set of fangs is used more for mutilating and eating rather than the common delicate neck work a vampire attempts.

7. Mutated vampiric mouths can take on many shapes and sizes, with a little help from science. This vampire jaw can actually detach from the skull and attack its victims from the side.

WHAT ARE THESE VAMPIRES OVERCOMPENSATING FOR?

If you're ever in the mood to check out some footage of some truly stunning sets of fangs, pop in a few of these fangophilia flicks. Each vampire has a mouth full of glimmering beauties so large you'd think they were trying to draw attention from elsewhere. Fangs: the vampire Ferrari.

Vampire Circus
Sylvia, *Lair of the White Worm*
Kah, *The Legend of the 7 Golden Vampires*
Dracula's brides, *Van Helsing*
Fright Night
Dwight Renfield, *The Night Flier*
Katrina, *Vamp*

---

many vampires prefer to leave their fangs bared at all times, but generally, when they're not in use, the fangs shrink back into the gums.

From here the retractable-fang look begins to vary depending on the bloodline and vampire preference. Some members of the undead species wield a double fang.[9] That's two sets of canines in the top half of the jaw. Others pair bottom and top fangs for extra fierceness, although the tendency to start looking like a bottle opener is possible. Usually whatever his maker has will be passed on down to the ward, but one quick stop in the dentist's chair and a vampire can change his smile entirely.

The Rattler

The vampires from the Southern Vampire Mysteries book series underwent an interesting translation from page to tele-

---

9 See Danica Talos from the film *Blade: Trinity*, Henry Fitzroy in *Blood Ties*, and the vampires from *The Dresden Files*.

vision (the series *True Blood*). The fangs designed for these vampires are possibly one of the more realistic combinations of nature and supernatural beasts. The fangs were based on the structural makeup of the rattlesnake jaw: The fangs are hidden from view behind the teeth and flick out when an adrenaline rush kicks in. This is what we like to call the "fang flick."

The teeth are covered in a saliva that contains vampire venom (more on venom later), which (depending on the vampire) is stored in a pouch near the cheeks or freely flows through the saliva.

Fangless Species

Vampires without fangs are much more common than you may think; in fact, some of the species most beloved by hard-core enthusiasts don't have a toothed spike to speak of. (So no, *Twilight* wasn't the first set of defanged vampires.) In fact, neither Béla Lugosi nor Frank Langella felt the need for excessive fang use and ditched the fake teeth for their famous interpretations of Count Dracula. It makes more sense in today's world to ditch the fangs and go for the more subtle approach.

But just because these vampires lost their teeth doesn't mean they lost any powers. Many of them still retain superior strength through-out their body (fists that can punch though torsos and jaws that can bite through steel), along with super speed and any other unseen mental abilities they may have been blessed with along the way.[10]

A Mouthful of Ugly

For every vamp with pearly white cuspids, there's another vamp with a mouth full of mismatched, yellowing, gangly fangs.

---

10 Examples of fangless vamps include *Near Dark, Heartstopper, The Hunger, Daughters of Darkness, Rise: The Blood Hunter,* the *Twilight* series, *The Forsaken,* and *Martin.*

The wretched mouths of the vampire kind are not just an easy joke for the paranormal bully, they're also one of the most diverse and interesting facets of the vampire anatomy. It's a veritable rainbow of depleted and deformed calcium all twisted and warped into different shapes. Truly these vampire smiles are an unappreciated art of diversification.[11]

The gangly grin finds its home predominantly among Villainous Vampires, and it's dangerous and rare to see some of these ancient grins out on the street. But seeing as some of the earliest vampires were suggested or represented in the media as having dilapidated fangs, seeing one in today's times is like jumping back in a time machine. It's almost impossible to describe all the horrendous delights of this type of fang: They can be long, spaced out, different sizes, broken, twisted, or sticking out the side of a vampire's mouth. But mind you, they're deadly, and this type of vampire has no desire to show you his fillings if he's not going to get a meal out of the exchange.

An interesting subsection under twisted fangs is mutated jaws. Again, mostly prevalent in Villainous Vampires, this strange anatomical quirk allows the entire jaw to expand or crack open in order for the vampire to feed. This can be seen in the Reaper vampires in *Blade II*, who used this scientific advantage to feed on other vampires. Unlike the feelings of pleasure often reported by those bitten by the typical fanged vampire, this type of feeding appears to be incredibly painful and invariably fatal for the victim (except in the case of the Reapers; anyone bitten by a Reaper immediately begins the transformation into one).

Dabbling in science and basic evolution has brought changes to the vampire species. Over time, we will see a more advanced

---

11 Examples of warped fangs include *Nosferatu*, *Fright Night*, *Subspecies*, *30 Days of Night*, and *Salem's Lot*.

breed of fangs, or perhaps the phasing out of canines altogether, as the author Guillermo del Toro suggests in his novel *The Strain*, in which viral vampires use stingers instead of their teeth to attack their victims.

Venom

Be it supernatural juice or a poisonous pathogen, vampires secrete a powerful substance that will turn you from human to immortal—unless they kill you first. This fluid is commonly called venom but can also be considered a virus. It's hard to make

VAMPIRES AND DRUGS

In the Southern Vampire books and TV spin-off series *True Blood*, the vampire drug-trafficking industry is booming, and humans get an ethereal high from ingesting V-Juice (vampire blood). But what happens when a vampire bites the neck of a pot head? Do mortal drugs even pack a kick for the undead?

All signs point to yes. The Count from Norman Spinrad's *Vampire Junkies* novel develops a mean heroin addiction after feeding on the blood of a junkie in New York City. In the *Preacher* comics, the vampire character Cassidy battled some pretty terrible drug dependency problems, going to some serious lows to get a fix. *Buffy's* Angelus spits out the blood of a Sunnydale High School swim team member, which we first suspect is due to steroid use, but later discover was something more mischievous flowing in his veins. Still, his reluctance to drink tainted blood proves that perhaps they are influenced by what they eat. More to the point, Spike in the *Buffy* episode "School Hard" explains that while at Woodstock he "fed off a flower person and spent the next six hours watching my hand move." It would seem, according to pop lore, that vampires can indeed be influenced by mind-altering drugs, and in some cases, snake venom.

too many generalizations regarding vampire venom because it has mutated so quickly and violently over the years.

Some believe that the less human blood a vampire drinks, the less potent his venom is. This has yet to be proven without fatal consequences. Others believe that certain strains of the vampire virus have diluted the venom so far as to allow vampires to bite their victims and not fully turn them without other measures coming into play (such as a full blood exchange). Whatever the reality is, be aware that in most cases, when you are exposed to vampire venom, it will take time to get it out of your system, unless you are unlucky enough to be infected by a rare strain that initiates a transformation immediately. Frankly, it is not worth the risk of seeing just how far your body can go before the venom begins breaking down your genetic makeup and turning your body.

Vampire Siring

Just like the spectrum of fangs seen in the vampire world, there's also a spectrum of ways that vampires turn humans. Most involve some sort of blood exchange with a vampire, but there are exceptions even to this rule, so it is important to be familiar with the various rituals so that you are prepared to defend yourself should you find yourself on the verge of being turned.

Swapping Blood Types

The most common vampire siring ceremony is the simple act of the vampire drinking from the human, and in exchange, the human drinking the vampire's blood. In most cases, humans will need to be drained of almost all of their blood, which will leave them in an intensely weakened state. If not fully drained, the humans, if they survive the blood loss, will remain mortal but will pick up a few nasty habits along the way (repulsion to sunlight, hissing, carnal thirst for blood). But in order for complete transformation mortals will most likely need to be placed on the brink of death, so that copious amounts of vampire blood can revive them into immortals. This practice is not particularly new; in fact it's been around since Bram Stoker's *Dracula*, *The Vampire Chronicles*, and even the modern-day *The Vampire Diaries*. The key to this transformation is that the mortal shell must, in a way, die, so the vampire can emerge.

Patience Is an Undead Virtue

A few turning rituals seem to take a lot of time, days even, and several blood exchanges. Southern vampire Bill Compton explained it best to girlfriend Sookie Stackhouse in *Dead Until Dark*: "I would have to drain you, at one sitting or over two or three days, to the point of your death, then give you my blood. You would lie like a corpse for about forty-eight hours, sometimes as long as three days, then rise and walk at night. And you would be hungry . . . Other vampires have told me humans they habitually bite, day after day, can become vampires quite unexpectedly. But that requires consecutive, deep, feedings. Others, under the same conditions, merely become anemic."

In the TV series *True Blood*, the maker and his ward are actually buried together in the ground while the process occurs. Burial is not uncommon, as the process takes time. Many midturns are actually considered dead by the human race and given a proper burial, only to emerge *Buffy*-style in the middle of a cemetery. Thankfully, the superhuman strength you'll gain from becoming a vamp should help you claw your way out of the dirty grave, as it did for the teenaged Gina Covella from *Vamped*, who woke up (surprise!) in a coffin.

Just a Bite

Some vamps need only one bite to make them yours. *Twilight* vamps work under this principle: Bella, when bitten, gyrates and flaps about on the ground, withering in pain from the vampire venom, well on her way to becoming a vamp after just one bite. But this isn't a new legend. The also-fangless vamps from *Near Dark* can turn a mortal to the fang with a simple nibble.

This Blood's for You

Be warned, siring blood doesn't always come from the neck, wrist, or sliced-up chest of an oversexed vampire. Sometimes it can come in the form of a bottle. *The Lost Boys* (in both I and II) tricked their new vampire gang members into sampling a little household wine. And by "wine" they meant ancient vampire blood that turns the unsuspecting, underage drinkers. Similarly, in *A Taste of Blood*, the main character is sent two bottles of Slivo-vitz brandy from an old ancestor, and after pounding through the drink, he becomes a vampire. So be wary when vials of mysterious liquids are being passed around a vampire party. That could be the one drink that puts you eternally over the edge.

Virus Versus Curse

A lot of people question how it's possible to reconcile the idea of a vampire who has evolved from a religious curse to the more scientific notion of "vampire mutation as virus" that we see in the media today. However, whatever the true reason, the ideas aren't mutually exclusive.

Before recent advances in modern science, the only plausible explanation for vampirism to most people was a supernatural curse. The various strains that do react adversely to religious arti-

VAMPIRE ANIMALS

People are not the only creatures who can fall under the fang. Rare and strange reports have been found in popular culture regarding many a mysterious Animal Vampire. Forget the adorable carrot juice–sucking rabbit Bunnicula—we're talking animals that go in for the kill. Possibly the most famous of animals turned vampire is Hell Cow, who was transformed by Dracula in the *Howard the Duck* comic book.

facts only seemed to confirm these beliefs.[12] But whether or not the initial trigger for the creation of the first vampire was mystical, these days the commonly accepted belief is that most vampires are infected with a virus that is present in the blood and transmittable to humans. As a scientist in *Blade II* explains, "Vampirism is a progressive virus that's spread through the saliva of various parasitic organisms." Such a theory also explains the potential for animals to be infected as well.[13]

This by no means disregards the notion that vampires are supernatural beings. The very fact that there is a viral strain that turns people into half-dead, bloodthirsty monsters is a magical thing, but hopefully, once we get a better and longer look at various specimens, we can have a better understanding of where vampires came from. We may find the boundaries of what's supernatural and what's science shrinking over the years thanks to technology.

12 Certainly in the *Buffy* universe, there is a strong religious element at play, as the vampire curse is described as unholy demons taking over the bodies of the human hosts and destroying their souls.

13 We've also seen the virus take pill form as represented in the Swedish film *Frostbiten*.

So remember, just because some people are infected with a nosferatu strain or vampire venom, that doesn't necessarily make them cursed by God—it may just make them very unlucky.

ABILITIES

Vampires are supernatural creatures, and when you start delving into what makes each of them unique and different, you're going to encounter a lot of variety. Like hair color in humans, vampiric special abilities vary widely. Some vamps are turned into psychics or gain the ability to glide upon transformation; others wake up in their new vampire life with just the bare necessities, like super strength and speed. We have determined that telekinetic powers *seem* to be class specific—you'll find more information on each class's ability in the following chapters. Beyond that, their abilities seem to be present across the board, and are most likely evolving rapidly.

CAN VAMPIRES FLY?

Vampire expert Anne Rice let her darling Lestat soar through the air, and Dracula has been reported to take on the form of a bat to frighten the ancient townspeople of Transylvania. But close examination of the myths, legends, and lore reveals that it is typically only the most powerful, oldest, and most influential vampires who possess the power of levitation. Perhaps this is because the younger vampiric generations' power has been diluted over time. Either way, who needs flight when you've got enough power in your body to scale rooftops and glide about like a superhero?

So could a common vampire walking the streets today take to the skies like a devil bird? Probably not, unless you're dealing with an ancient evil, or a creature that can transform into an animal.

Vampire GPS

One useful talent possessed by vampires is their internal GPS.

Vampires rarely get lost or need directions. Their life on the road comes naturally, as their minds are programmed to be aware of their whereabouts even in their sleep. This makes long traveling days in a car with blacked-out windows much easier. Who needs rearview mirrors when you can sense the environment all around you?

Vamps employ this ability through their lackeys and those they've bitten. When a vampire bites into a human, he has made a connection, and can therefore keep tabs (rather creepily) on his surroundings as well as his lunch (these human servants are often referred to as *familiars*).

This internal GPS is also a fantastic security alarm. It's a rare and almost impossible feat to sneak up on a vampire. Vamps have usually made a few enemies in the course of their undead existence, whether they've made mistakes and lashed out in anger or hunger, or they've decided to crusade against their own kind as the Tragic Hero. Either way, keeping a safe perimeter is always important, and vampires' heightened senses and internal awareness keep them continually informed of their surroundings.[14]

WEAKNESSES

Sunlight

Even though we've all seen and heard about the vampires who walk in the day, generally speaking, most vampires experience a strong

---

14 Vampires who use people as homing devices are seen in the Sookie Stackhouse series, the *Twilight* series, Bram Stoker's *Dracula*, *Dracula 2000*, *The Forsaken*, and *The Vampire Chronicles* (though these vamps are usually using one another).

THE SPARKLE FACTOR

As of late, there has been great debate surrounding the sunlight factor and its effect on the epidermis of a vampire; yes, we're speaking of the "real vampires don't sparkle" controversy surrounding the *Twilight* vamps.

So, do some vampires sparkle in the sun? Because most pop culture myths have some basis in historical fact, it's a possibility. But in the end it's difficult to say. There are no ancient myths of glittering vampires, although we do know that some species of vamps can freely stroll about in the daytime. The stance on sparkle is going to have to remain in the air until more than one pop culture outlet can agree that vampires have mutated, evolved, or always retained the glimmering ability.

immunological resistance to sunlight. Most vamps begin to crackle, pop, and simmer under UV rays, and if overexposed they can literally burst into a mess. Disregarding liberally applied suntan lotion, spells, and the off chance that they've stumbled upon an ancient protective ring,[15] almost all vampires are subject to discomfort at the least and immolation at the worst when in range of the sun.[16]

15 There seems to be a world of accessories available to vampirekind that allows them to wander into the daylight. In *The Vampire Diaries*, Stefan and Damon wear lapis lazuli rings that allow them into the morning light. In *Buffy the Vampire Slayer*'s "The Harsh Light of Day," Spike uncovers the Gem of Amarra, a ring that makes him immune to things like staking, light, and garlic. Angel later gets his hands on the gem as a gift from his ex. But not all vampire rings will help you. Use caution when you're playing with the trinkets of the undead. The is best demonstrated when Maximillian's ring is placed on another in *Vampire in Brooklyn*. The bling instantly transforms the wearer into a vampire, with some below-the-belt assets (at least it's not all bad).

16 However, vampire detective Mick St. John of *Moonlight* was shockingly able to walk into the desert with a hat and sunglasses for some time until he eventually lost his will because of overexposure.

Stakes

The seemingly most reliable way to end a vampire pest problem is a stake, or "Mr. Pointy" as it's so lovingly called in the *Buffy* series. A sharp wooden stake to the heart means immediate death for just about all vampires, minus a few Big Bads who may need a little nudging from other vampire-be-gone tricks. Also, as some vampires react poorly to silver, a silver stake can be twice as deadly in some cases.

Religious Paraphernalia

Crosses, holy water, priests, and blessings—back in the days of old, this was all a human needed to keep a nosferatu at bay. Take note: Those days are gone.

When religion was the government and vice versa, it was easy to peddle religious signs as believable weapons against evil. Why wouldn't people look for defense from something they find solace in?

However, in most cases today, vampires have seemingly begun to build up an immunity to such religious symbols. More and more we're seeing new crops of vampires who aren't stopped in their tracks at the sight of the cross; instead, they're only made uncomfortable or irritated. The well-placed cross here and there has still managed to burn a few vampire hands, but it's not going

CAN A VAMPIRE CROSS A RIVER?

Although ancient vampires still seem to be put off by the river crossing, today's vampires are either not bothered at all by this old superstition or just slightly weakened (a perfect example being *The Vampire Diaries*, where more powerful vampires are the only ones affected by crossing running water). This is similar to the no-longer-as-potent religious mediums.

to shield you from a supernatural right hook. That being said, ancient undiluted evil still manages to feel at least some effects from these past religious defense mechanisms. So should you put all your trust behind a bottle of holy water? No, but that doesn't mean it's not worth a shot. If anything, it may cause enough annoyance to allow you the opportunity to escape.

Human Food

Vampires are a finicky lot; giving up their diet of blood seems to have different effects on every vampire. For example, when Andy

VEGAN VAMPS

Whether a taste preference, dietary issue, or moral choice, **many vampires go vegan, forsaking human blood and opting for a less dangerous dinner, whether it be animal blood or a synthetic replacement. The world of vegan vampirism is thriving.**

These days, it seems like everyone is claiming to be a vegan vampire, but the reality of the situation is, if the vampire is drinking human blood, be it from blood packets, banks, or consenting donors, they're not technically a "vegan" vampire. Instead they're more of a "restricted diet" vamp.

In *Vampires Anonymous*, a telephone and sponsored program are offered for vamps that are ready to kick the human habit. There's even a test to determine what type of animal blood they'd prefer; in the main character's case, it turns out to be sheep. Jeremy Capello from *My Best Friend Is a Vampire* is seen with cases of canned pigs' blood; Boya from *Blood & Donuts* feasts on local city creatures—pigeons and rats; and the Southern Vampire series and related TV show *True Blood* feature the booming market of Tru Blood, a synthetic blood beverage for vampires. The Cullens from the Twilight series battle their blood-lust daily and hunt animals for blood in the forest. Stefan Salvatore from *The Vampire Diaries* attempts to stick to animal blood as well.

Warhol's protagonist in *Blood for Dracula* strays from his strict diet of virginal blood only (or is lied to about the status of a victim's chastity), it's a blood-filled trip to the toilet for him, face first. Yet other vampires (*The Vampire Diaries, Fright Night*) have little to no problem ingesting human food, though it offers them zero nutritional value. Clearly this is a bloodline issue, and it's best to ask before cooking up a meal and expecting rave reviews from a member of the undead.

Invitation Inside

It seems that whether old or new, most vampires still hold true to the ancient belief that they must be invited into a home before entering. The question of what will happen if a vampire enters an abode without the permission of the owner first was answered quite gruesomely in *Let the Right One In*, which showed the Child Vampire Eli hemorrhaging blood from every orifice. But like all things *Twilight*, it would seem that rules are meant to be broken in this world and open windows are ripe for creepy nighttime watch sessions, invitation or no.

CAN YOU TAKE A VAMPIRE'S PICTURE?

Usually yes, but only with a digital camera for some. The use of silver in past camera processing stopped most vampiric images from showing up on film, so says *Moonlight*'s Mick St. John. The urban legend about photographs presumably stems from the mirror myth, which holds that you can't see vampires in a mirror. Many vampires suffer from a lack of a reflection, but it seems that it is bloodline specific; the Maker passes it down to his or her vampire children and so forth, which means that while some vampires can have their pictures taken and will appear in the reflection of a mirror, others cannot.

2

ROMANTIC
VAMPIRES

HEMOPHAGE ROMANORUM

"You are my life now," he answered simply.

—Edward, *Twilight*

Arguably the most famous class of pop culture vampire is the Romantic Vampire. These days, *Hemophage romanorum* has the most loyal and dedicated stream of fans, thanks to the media's obsession with vampires in love. The intense popularity of this classification has led many a human on the hunt for that gaunt, misunderstood vampire lover who awaits "the one."

The typical portrayal of the Romantic Vampire in the media, however, leaves people utterly unprepared for interaction with the real volatile deal. This specific class of vampire is often abused and neglected, harbors deep-seated issues about his past, and most likely was a participant in a bloody massacre or two.

Skipping merrily into this type of vamp's embrace without an education on what's exactly behind those big shiny eyes can end poorly for both parties involved if the interaction is not handled with care. Should things turn foul, knowing how to identify, approach, and politely exit a Romantic Vampire encounter improves your chances of emerging unscarred.

FROM CAPE TO COUTURE:
PHYSICAL IDENTIFIERS

Attire

Romantic Vamps are meticulously groomed. Expect their eyebrows to be plucked, faces washed, nails cleaned, and lips pursed (as well as questionably glossy), and the subject to be expertly accessorized. Call it a necessity of evolution or merely another way to lure in unsuspecting prey, but vampires in the Romantic category are devoted to the ever-changing tides of fashion and love to primp themselves with the best of threads and trinkets.

The vampire fervor for fashion is so well known that many corporations have shelled out the big bucks to capture that immortal demographic.[1] Attire can be a key facet in identifying a suspected vampire on the hunt for another love victim. You won't see a Romantic Vamp traipsing around late-night haunts in a woolly "Cosby" sweater or last season's corduroy jacket. Poor attire draws negative attention from both the public and, more important, a desired mate. A fashion faux pas can become a telltale sign that this being is not of the here and now, and if so, the vamp will ditch it. No matter how sentimental the clothing item

---

1 Ray-Ban is a classic example of vampire marketing. Starting from when the character Michael prominently wore a pair of shades similar to Ray-Ban's Clubmasters line on the movie poster for *The Lost Boys*, the company began to pay attention to the vampire audience. In the late 1990s, Ray-Ban started to advertise its super-strength sunglasses line specifically to vampires. A smart move, as you can see that ad campaign's influence even today in the exceedingly popular media representation of the Romantic Vampire; *Twilight*'s Edward Cullen's daytime strutting, for example, is not complete without his Ray-Ban Wayfarers.

Romantic Vampires

Hemophage romanorum

might be, survival comes first.[2] Rest assured that Romantic Vampires, fictional or not, will stow away such goods for safekeeping or the second coming (waste not, want not).

True Romantic Vamps naturally look like they belong among the upper echelon of any society without lifting even a well-manicured finger. Their look appears, above all things, classic yet modern. They seem to have stepped out of the pages of a fashion magazine with an effortless and beautiful leap.

That being said, do be wary when dealing with a supposed immortal who's still sporting a "Frankie Say Relax" shirt, because you most likely have a poser or a misguided Villain on your hands. Either way, get out of the situation immediately because the only thing worse than dealing with a vampire wannabe is crossing paths with a Villainous Vamp who hasn't had a good meal since George Michael was in Wham!

MADE FOR LOVIN':
PHYSICAL FEATURES

Even though Romantic Vampires are choosy about their street attire, this in no way means the lovelorn vampire should be dismissed as a foppish creature unworthy of your respect. The finicky mannerisms hardly mask the genetic advantage this vampire classification has in terms of sexual appeal. Their physical allure is formidable even to the mightiest of Villainous Vamps—not to mention that it makes them practically irresistible to the rest of us mere mortals. When dealing with the Romantic Vampire, be

---

2 Even *Buffy's* Angel had to upgrade from his shiny leathers to tailored button-downs.

aware of what is real and what is purely Mother Nature playing with your carnal desires.

Skin

One seduction tool in the Romantic Vampire's repertoire is the skin. Romantic Vampires have no need for mortal exfoliation, under-eye cream, or even lotion; they don't wrinkle with age or look worn down (unless they haven't eaten, but even that is easily remedied). Once created, they're gifted with a flawless complexion that only grows more marble-esque over the years. Although their exterior may be cold to the touch, it has a pleasing feel to it. The beauty of their unblemished cheeks calls out to mortals, but like the smooth lines of an ancient Roman statue, it's best not to touch.

The full turning doesn't just stop with blemishes, bags, and wrinkles. Some pop culture vampire chroniclers believe that the vampiric cure-all kiss of eternal life will replace missing parts of flesh and scars. The perfect pop culture example is from Christopher Moore's *You Suck*, in which the turning ritual also returned body bits below the belt that were once surgically removed. Vampire Tommy wakes up to find himself brand new, as his previous circumcision has been reverted. So it sounds like a bris can quite possibly be undone.

Eyes

Nothing is as captivating as holding a vampire's gaze. Forget mind control; just the color change an immortal's iris goes through will leave you stunned and speechless (see Common Vampire Eye Colors on page 13). The media has always paid specific attention to the eyes of the Romantic Vampire. When a Villainous

Vampire has a victim under his thrall, the color of the evil being's eyes is mentioned, but not harped upon. But when dealing with a Romantic Vampire, the love victim is often found mesmerized and trapped in gold hues, ice-blue tints, or frightening reds. Perhaps the excessive attention paid to this class's eyes is simply because very few other classifications of vampire would let mortals so close and allow them to live to tell of it.

First and foremost, Romantic Vampires use the eyes to hold one's attention. This allows them to drone on about their loveless life or sorrows without seeming like they're telling any old sob story. The other and far more publicized ability of the vampire stare is its seductive draw. Although many Villains charm their prey with deceptive behavior, the Romantics continue to seduce, albeit ever so lightly, with the eyes. One of the earliest records of such sexual seduction through vampiric gaze is Lord Ruthven, who is often credited with making vampires "sexy." Next in line as the vampire sex icon is Béla Lugosi's Dracula, who, by today's standards, would be considered a Romantic Vampire.[3]

Although a Tragic Vampire or even a Villainous Vamp can strike terror and fear into a victim's heart with a mere blink of the eyelid, Romantic Vampires can keep their love victims spell-

---

3 Granted, Dracula never had the purest of love intentions, but his gaze was known to sexually excite even the most decent of women: From the 1931 *Dracula* with Helen Chandler as Mina: "When the dream came, it seemed the whole room was filled with mist. It was so thick, I could just see the lamp by the bed, a tiny spark in the fog. And then I saw two red eyes glaring at me. And a white livid face came down out of the mist. It came closer and closer. I felt its breath on my face and then its lips . . . oh!" Dracula has always straddled the Romantic, Villainous, and Tragic classifications, but the Lugosi representation is an exceedingly large influence on the portrayal of Romantic Vampires today. This is a classic example of the old seductive gaze; notice the "oh!"

bound and randy for hours, without the use of much mind control. Call it a reflection of the Romantics' desire or pure sexual chemistry; it's one of the Romantics' most effective techniques for a love encounter.

Fangs

You can't separate sex and fangs when it comes to the Romantic Vampire.[4] Whether you're partaking in the pleasures of the flesh or abstaining, when a fanged vampire gets sexually excited, you'll most likely be facing two pointy pearly whites.

Although vampires can openly release their fangs during sexual stimulation (both mentally and physically), it is a personal preference. Some Romantic Vamps are embarrassed by Mother Nature's warning sign. These particular nosferatu are normally exceedingly skilled in the art of self-control. A vampire can learn how to control the telltale sign of excitement so as to not frighten off a possible mate or date.

The actual fangs of Romantic Vamps are similar to the creature: delicate and chic, but deadly. When talking to a Romantic Vampire, if you're privy to a "fang slip," it's best to steer the conversation away from flirtatious talk or you may find yourself an unwilling volunteer for vampiric infatuation.

Excluding the fangless breeds, *Hemophage romanorum*'s chompers normally fall into two categories. The first is a set of

4 Note, however, that the presence or absence of fangs is not enough information alone to classify a Romantic Vampire. Many examples of the species do not have fangs, or they file their teeth down to blend in. But even Romantic Vamps with the dullest teeth have the jaw power to bite through just about any object, and when the sexual bloodlust is upon them, your arteries will look mighty appealing.

canines quite similar to the rattlesnake reptile (see figure 1 on page 15). The front set of fangs can flick out if the vamp is excited, angry, or scared.[5]

The second set of fangs common to the Romantics appears to grow out of the gum line, located in the front of the mouth (see figure 3 on page 15.)

The release of the fangs puts the vampire in a heightened level of sensual awareness, opening up an ultrasensitive pathway in the mouth that directly connects to the pleasure center of the brain.

Nails

The Romantic Vampire can be easily identified through its hands and nails. Romantic Vamps' fingers are longer than those of a normal human's. Their nails will also be slightly longer, but not ghoulish or threatening. Look for delicate yet powerful hands with glimmering fingernails—even on the males.[6] If they shine like glass and cut the flesh, you've got someone who is Romantic but living-challenged.

Hair

Although many physical characteristics of the Romantic Vampire are a lovely sight to behold, the tragic flaw of this class is a lack of discerning taste for hairstyles. From their earliest incarnations,

---

5 *True Blood*, the television series based on the Charlaine Harris novels, created the most accurate representation of the "snake fang" vampire. The production crew modeled the look directly after a rattlesnake, which is about as close as you'll get to the inside of a vampire's mouth without scars.

6 Anne Rice was dead-on when describing her vampires as having nails similar to glass throughout her *Vampire Chronicles*.

Romantic Vamps have carried questionable coiffures atop their heads. It first started with a general misuse of hair product.[7] From the 1930s to the 1950s, there was a veritable clan of grease tops who shoveled hair gel down their slicked-back skulls.

The 1980s saw a renaissance of strong widow's peaks on most lovesick undead. Although many members continued to support the greased-back style, other immortals opted for bleach abuse. The general need for vampire conditioner hit alarming heights in the 1980s, but vampires continued to bleach and grease their heads.[8]

The 1990s brought in a period of heavily gooed and spiked 'dos,[9] shortly followed by the modern-day combination of hair goop and not showering that we see so often today.[10] This is one of those rare media representations of a classification that seems to have hit the nail on the coffin, so to speak.

You could argue that unfortunate hair choices span across the vampire classifications, but it truly seems to make its most awful mark on the Romantics, a fact noticed, perhaps, because they're otherwise so perfectly groomed. Even the poor vampire souls doomed to a life with the exact same cut they had when they were sired contribute to the terrible hair phenomenon.

---

7 Captured perfectly on film thanks to the slicked-back 'do modeled by actor Béla Lugosi.

8 See the entire cast of *The Lost Boys*.

9 Angel's foe/sometime ally Spike often disparages Angel's hair, referring to the "nancy-boy hair gel" he uses. Not that Billy Idol–tressed Spike has any room to criticize.

10 See Cullen, Edward.

HOME SWEET COFFIN AND OTHER HANGOUTS:
HABITAT

Residence

Romantic Vampires usually have the most "human-friendly" abodes. This is a species on the lookout for love, and even if they live in a crypt or run-down shack, the interior will be more than comfortable. Most prefer a classic style with antiquities from their past surrounding them for comfort. The popular image of a swanky bachelor pad with red walls, velvet furniture, and an overly seductive gothic style is more media hype than reality. But as far as specific locations that appeal to the amorous vampires, this type could appear in various real estate situations and even have roommates.[11]

Proper etiquette when entering a Romantic Vampire's home is not to look for a coffin. Visitors shouldn't inquire as to its existence or ask to actually see it; both questions are considered very forward. In fact, many vampires have evolved past the "security blanket" of a coffin. If a particular vampire is not dependent on certain ground or a pine box, he will retreat to a comfy bed. Still, the C-word is a delicate subject for all vampires, especially those trying to cavort among the living. No one can be truly sure whether the vampire in question still sleeps in the traditional wooden box or bed, so it's best to keep one's mouth zipped about the matter at hand.

Should a vampire trade bedclothes for the traditional coffin, expect it to be just as comfortable as a bed in a box, but still

---

11 The BBC series *Being Human* wasn't terribly off with the idea of a vampire, a ghost, and a werewolf sharing a flat in Bristol.

simple. Vampires are often pulled into a dark slumber, so fitting one's coffin with TVs, stereos, and nightlights is considered frivolous at best.

If you are one of the few living beings who actually gets to view the private and locked-away coffin resting place of a Romantic Vampire, consider yourself lucky: You are obviously close enough to an immortal who not only trusts you but hasn't killed you. (Luckily, you won't have to sleep in there, as even Romantic Vamps aren't particularly keen on sharing something as intimate as a coffin.)

Haunts

The undead world's eternal lover is surprisingly easy to spot if you know where to go. Don't waste your time on something as obvious as a "vampire bar"[12]—nothing turns off an immortal Romantic faster than poseur vamps.

Instead, check out cultural festivities on the cusp of society: rock concerts, hidden bars, cozy cafés, and other small venues. Think small, intimate, and cutting edge. Most Romantic Vampires have had decades to cultivate a specific taste for talent, so they know what will be the next big wave in art, literature, and music, and they flock to things of beauty like moths to a flame. Plus these are great places to meet others, and what's sexier than running into a hundred-year-old expert on something you share an interest in?

On that same note, should the artist in question retain any of these physical traits and possess a moody demeanor, you may want to ask him how old he is. The common attitude and embrace

---

12 Although they may run "authentic" vampire bars, most Romantic Vamps are in it for profit and the occasional snack. See Fangtasia in the Southern Vampire Mystenes.

of an avant-garde lifestyle allows the casual vampire to slip in every once in a while.

WHAT YOU DON'T KNOW CAN HURT YOU:
UNSEEN ABILITIES

Heightened Senses

Like most creatures of the night, the Romantic Vampires are blessed with supremely acute senses. In fact, many vamps going through a Romantic lifestyle change use these abilities in more new and interesting ways than other classes do. No more stalking your prey with your excellent senses in the middle of the woods— now they can use their skills to stalk the perfect companion at a local haunt. Before you've even ordered a drink, Romantic Vampires are aware if you need something refreshing or warm by sensing your body temperature. They can hear what you're murmuring to your friends and see your cheeks fill with blood when your eyes meet. The application of the heightened senses makes the social hunter completely prepared to meet your every whim. This, in turn, makes Romantic Vampires appear beyond perfect and exceptionally considerate, which is exactly what they want you to think.

Remember, just about everything is a scam to get you to be their new love slave or companion. The things you may consider advantageous upon a new encounter will later come back to bite you in the rear. Imagine having a companion who can track your every desire, even when you don't want him to—*annoying* is hardly the word when you're deflecting a full-blown jealousy attack for merely blushing at a stranger's compliment.

Pheromones

Like humans, vampires are capable of emitting a smell that will attract and allure others to their side. Should you get a nose full of undead Romantic Vamp pheromones, remain calm; step away and take deep breaths. By all means, resist the urge to dance with the pale creature giving you bedroom eyes from across that room. Dancing with Romantic Vampires is the ultimate act of seductive intimacy, yet they never seem to take into consideration their desired conquest's feelings on the matter. The pursuer will delight in making you his musical puppet, picking you up and twirling you around, or, worse, busting out a full-fledged choreographed dance-off in the middle of your high school prom. In fact, should you know there is a vampire after you, it's best to avoid any sort of location where dancing will take place unless you want to become the unwilling pawn in a synchronized disco dance-off. There are multiple documentations of this happening, and it never looks as good as you think it does from the outside.[13]

It's with good self-awareness that *Buffy*'s Angel claims he "doesn't dance," as nine out of ten vampires fail at the act, and the exceptions end up looking like blood-covered fools gyrating to Pump Panel Reconstruction's "Confusion" (or as it's better known, the bloodbath club scene from *Blade*).

---

13 Classic examples from the media of the vampire pheromone dance include a Halloween high school dance-off turned strip show to "Hands Off" in *Once Bitten, Fright Night*'s vampy club seduction dance to "Good Man in a Bad Time," an unholy ballroom dance between Dracula and poorly accented Kate Beckinsale in *Van Helsing*, and a disco two-step to "I Love the Nightlife" in *Love at First Bite* (though the song was strangely removed from the VHS and DVD releases and replaced with an unknown disco tune—staking the moment entirely).

On the flip side, you should never watch a vampire dance, as it involves a deadly combination of vampiric pheromone release, eye contact, and subtle mind control. Should a vampire begin to dance in front of you, look away or else you'll be a helpless lapdog lover to a vampire looking for some extra attention or perhaps a snack. Female vampires, both Villainous and good natured, are notorious for the intoxicating dance of seduction.[14]

Mind Control

The ability to control or read a mortal's thoughts varies from vampire to vampire. But with amorous vampires specifically, you won't be witnessing a Hammer Films display of mind control. In fact most Romantics are loath to use the forceful mind freeze over a person because there's no thrill in it. The real issue with *Hemophage romanorum*'s mind-control powers comes when dealing with a human's enhanced connections to telekinesis.

A person's ability to read the thoughts of others or to block outsiders from reading his mind is a hot draw for Romantic Vampires. Vampires looking for a mate often tire of the basic human mind, and searching for something new can take centuries. When a member of the undead happens upon someone with the power to read or block minds, there can be an immediate attraction.[15]

---

14 The vampire queen Santanico Pandemonium (as portrayed by Salma Hayek in *From Dusk Till Dawn*) used her smooth moves to great effect in entrancing patrons of the local trucker hangout. However, she proceeded to eat them all, cementing her final classification as a Villain rather than a Romantic Vampire.

15 Both Sookie Stackhouse and Bella Swan are perfect examples of humans with special telekinetic powers that appeal to Romantic Vampires. Sookie cannot read the mind of Bill Compton or Eric Northman and thus finds them appealing and easy to be around (a new human reaction for the aged beasts!). Edward Cullen

It would seem that Romantic Vampires aren't so worried about possessing the mind of a human; rather they are more attracted to those unique minds that can challenge their lives or alter their experiences with the human world. Also, charming vamps on the lookout for affection hardly need to tap into mind control when they have so many other assets going for them.

If for whatever reason you find yourself joined in mind with a Romantic Vampire, expect it to be a very invasive experience. These types of vamps hold a lot of pride in their chosen alternative lifestyle and overall restraint while consorting so closely with humans. If you present a challenge to them, especially in a matching of wits, they will not stop until they're satisfied. Exceptional differences such as telekinesis will draw out a lot of curious vamps looking for a new thrill.

Shape-Shifting

Some specific breeds of the Romantics do possess the ability to shape-shift. Anytime you see a young lady dancing in a cloud of mist, chances are the mist is a Romantic Vampire in gaseous form. Seven out of ten reports of a wolf "miraculously escaping the zoo" are actually careless Romantic Vamps who let themselves be seen trotting through city streets still in animal form.

The Romantic will change form only in a manner that aids in seduction. If it's a fanged and winged rat attacking your hair, or a mass of insects scuttling about on the floor, you're not dealing with a Romantic Vamp.

---

cannot read Bella's thoughts but is immediately intrigued by her, perhaps for this very reason.

STAKE HIS HEART OR BREAK IT?
ROMANTIC VAMPIRE BEHAVIOR

Even with all their overly passionate flaws, Romantic Vampires love with all of their being. If they don't become borderline obsessive, there's a chance for a true and long relationship, provided they never lash out and eat you for lunch. But if they did, it's certain they'd feel awful about it the next day.

VAMPIRES AND HOMOSEXUALITY

Vampires are a forward-thinking and tolerant species, and the homosexual lifestyle was embraced within the vampire community centuries ago. The vampire that broke down the coffin door for the rest of the gay vampiric world is the legendry Carmilla from the novella of the same name by Joseph Sheridan Le Fanu (inspired by Samuel Taylor Coleridge's poem "Christabel"). In fact, "Carmilla," published in 1872, was around before Dracula ever hit his popular stride.

The story introduced the world to the exceedingly beautiful and sexual female vampire whose victims were other women. This novella has inspired countless female vampire works and set the bar high for future leading vampire ladies.

Besides a few minor characters, like the sadly foppish Herbert who, in a bout of homoerotic slapstick, tries to seduce Roman Polanski's Albert in *Fearless Vampire Killers*, it is Anne Rice who is known best for her questionably androgynous vampire characters, including Louis and Lestat. But Rice keeps the act of blood drinking more central in her vampire franchise than sexual acts of any nature.

Characters such as these have paved the way for vampiric love of any kind. It also opened the door to a lot of vampire sexploitation films, such as *The Hunger*, *Vampire Ecstasy*, and the cheeky *Lesbian Vampire Killers*.

WHAT TO DO IF APPROACHED

If you are chosen to be a Romantic Vampire's companion, you'll be approached with one thought and one thought only in mind: How can he have you immediately?

What the definition of *have* is remains to be seen. You could be getting seduced by a three-way happy vampire who needs your sexin' to survive,[16] or you could be romanced by a vampire who has soulmated with you and is ready to spend the rest of eternity together.[17] Either way, nobody is getting out of this conversation without stepping into a big pile of vampire intensity.

If you are singled out by a Romantic Vampire seeking sexual or spiritual sacrifice, the best way to stave off these advances is to feign or just show indifference. Politely ignoring their advances is the best way to exit out of a vampire meet-and-greet when he's launched into a long, passion-filled exposé about his feelings.

Warning: Do not say you are with another vampire, as this will only make things much worse. Jealousy is like gasoline on a fire to Romantic Vampires. Don't play the jealousy card unless you have the goods to back it up. Even then, it's usually not worth it.

If the honest approach doesn't work, feigning or showing annoyance is the best way to leave unscarred. Turn the emotional tables on them, talk about your feelings, rant; these vampires are anything if not polite and hate to have inconvenienced you. Additionally, appearing whiny and self-absorbed knocks you off the perfection pedestal they're trying to put you on; Romantic

---

16 See Jean-Claude from the Anita Blake, Vampire Hunter series.

17 See any of the members of J. R. Ward's Black Dagger Brotherhood or Christine Feehan's Carpathians.

ROMANTIC VAMPIRE ATTACK WARNING SIGNS

Should you find yourself in conversation with a vampire in love, know what to look for in case of trouble:

- The baring of teeth, in a smile or frown (fanged or not fanged)
- If the vampire can't stop laughing, but won't share the joke
- All of a sudden your top's off
- Feeling dizzy or lightheaded
- Eye contact has been switched to neck contact
- Stomach growls from the vamp
- A shaking hand (usually means his restraint is faltering)
- Lip licking without or before lip locking

Vampires like to think they're attracted only to the cream of the crop, not a garden-variety human.

If this tactic also fails, determine whether he is a daylight-sensitive vampire (see page 25) and keep the sunshine on your side, never meeting at night. You can kill most Romantic Vampires with a stake in the heart or decapitation, but this is a close-range attack method. It is in your best interest never to get super close to any vamp whom you deem a possible bite threat.

Crucifixes, holy water, and garlic are wholly unreliable and hard to depend on; it's best to avoid a terrible scene and not take the risk of brandishing a worthless method of defense.

HEMOPHAGE ROMANORUM:
KNOWN SPECIMENS

Known examples of the Romantic Vampire fall into a variety of subcategories. These include the following:

Obsessed and Compulsive

They may be cute, but when they meet someone they like, it's all over. These vampires maintain a balancing act of stalker, monster, and devoted lover. Don't get involved unless you're ready to practically sign away your entire life. However, what this type lacks in independence, they make up for in the undead sack. No matter how you slice it, this vampire, once you get the chastity belt of morals out of the way, is undead dynamite in bed.

Known Specimens
Edward Cullen, *Twilight*
Bill Compton, the Southern Vampire Mysteries
Stefan Salvatore, *The Vampire Diaries*
Alex, *Tale of a Vampire*

In Love with Love

This particular vampire is more in love with the idea of a relationship and enjoys the contact high from the new lover more than the person herself. Don't tether your heart to one of these vamps; they will leave you the second they become bored or think you rely on them. These lotharios, though good for a little fun, have little concern with mortal issues, so you may end up sacrificing a lot of your personal time thanks to one of their many mood-swingy ideas. Just remember: If you get swept up in the idea of journeying to Venice with your new vampire squeeze, make sure he doesn't leave you there for another at the end of the night.

Known Specimens
Armand, *The Vampire Chronicles*
Marius, *The Vampire Chronicles*

Jean-Claude, the Anita Blake, Vampire Hunter series
Eric Northman (when he has his memory), the Southern
  Vampire Mysteries

Devoted and Disorderly

This troubled vampire soul usually comes from a rough past, which means lots of weighty issues for the two of you to work out together. Don't worry; they usually do their best thinking on their backs. Still, this breed of Romantic is loyal but troubled. You'll spend days trying to crack their hard outer shell after sifting through all the terrible things they've done in the past. This type of unruly love usually stems from deep passion and can awaken a whole lotta beast from your love that they thought they had buried years ago.

Known Specimens
Spike, *Buffy the Vampire Slayer*
Damon Salvatore, *The Vampire Diaries*
Lestat, *The Vampire Chronicles*

Looking for Love for All the Wrong Reasons

There's nothing wrong with wanting to be loved, unless that's all you're in a relationship for. There's a whole branch of Romantic Vampires simply moping about looking for someone to fill the gaping void in their life brought on by murder, sadness, and self-hatred. These vampires can also get exceedingly clingy but are still good for a romp. They're more interested in finding a mortal soul savior who can help them forgive themselves rather than a mate.

Known Specimens
Louis de Pointe du Lac, *The Vampire Chronicles*
Nick Knight, *Forever Knight*
Mitchell, *Being Human*

The Real Thing

The real deal. Love, trust, and understanding comes with these vampires. They may be a bit broken or rough around the edges, but their heart is always in the right place, even if their fangs may not be. Sadly, this is the rarest type of Romantic Vampire.

Known Specimens
Esme Cullen, *Twilight*
Carlisle Cullen, *Twilight*
Angel, *Buffy the Vampire Slayer*
Mick St. John, *Moonlight*
Mae, *Near Dark*

3

VILLAINOUS
VAMPIRES

HEMOPHAGE SCELERATUS

I told you, I feed erratically, and often enormously.

—Max Schreck, *Shadow of the Vampire*

As the predominant scourge of the supernatural under-world, Villainous Vampires are a serious force to be reckoned with. Be they scantily clad or fully robed, this classification has one, and only one, thing in mind: blood—specifically yours.

Although many other hemophages struggle with controlling their bloodlust, this kind embraces their carnal desire, making them the most dangerous of all the classifications, but in turn their evolutionary aptitude for hunting also makes them one of the most interesting species. This group's dissimilation from society has allowed them to grow uniquely as a specific type of hunter. Various vamps have even stopped evolving all together in certain areas where other types have flourished (for example, a few Villainous Vamps no longer have the ability to grow hair because blending in with society isn't an evolutionary priority to said vampire).

The most important things to remember when dealing with

this class is that you are nothing more than a meal, and their evil-doing has long passed the mustache-twirling stereotypes from long ago (though don't discount a bit of parlor room villainy antics). Never let your guard down around this type of vamp or you could be his next unwilling blood donor.

THE ORIGINAL SINNERS

Before they lived in our books and on our screens, vampire legends were passed down by word of mouth. While many parts of the world had their own vampire lore and gruesome ways to beat the beasts, there was hardly a kind word for any of these bloodsuckers. Most of them were described as reanimated corpses and were met with such fear that it caused a veritable corpse exhuming, beheading, and burning palooza in the eighteenth century in Eastern Europe.

One of the oldest and most popular tales of Villainous Vampire attacks happened in Kisolova, Serbia, in 1828. A villager named Peter Plogojowitz died and was buried, but according to the lore he returned to his house three days after his burial, hungry and looking for his son. Two days after that he reappeared again, and the next day his son was found dead. The citizens of Kisolova were suddenly being attacked and falling ill from loss of blood, and all claimed that Plogojowitz had bitten them on the neck. Eventually the town had enough and exhumed the body, finding him with eyes open, looking not-so-dead, and breathing ever so slightly. On his mouth was fresh blood. The townspeople drove a stake through his heart and burned the body.

Stories like this popped up all over the world. Someone dies, they come back, more people die, time to dig up and destroy the body. This vampire rumor mill only added fire to the vampire hysteria that would take us all the way through to today.

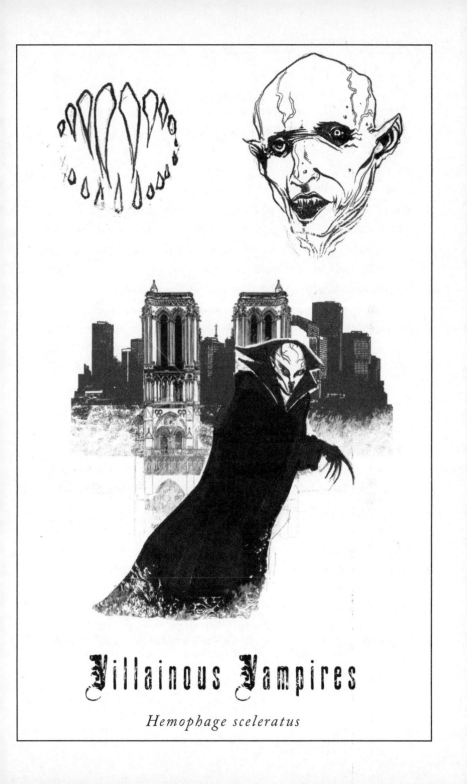

Villainous Vampires

Hemophage sceleratus

THAT'S A LOT OF VAMPIRIC LOOK:
PHYSICAL IDENTIFIERS

Attire

The most blatant "tell" for the deadliest of vampires is easily the hideous, dated, or over-the-top trimmings baddie vamps adorn themselves with. Although loners and Romantics are praised for their grasp of modern-day attire, these particular knaves are, as vampire slayer Jack Crow[1] would say, "fashion victims." Okay, maybe he was a bit harsher, but you get the picture.

The list of crimes against fashion by evil vampires is long. Sadly, all attempts to make a Villainous Vampire trendy would fall on deaf ears. This is a proud bunch, and they're not going to waste time fretting about trying to fit in. They do not care, nor will they lower themselves for human or even Romantic Vampire approval. Think of *Hemophage sceleratus* as a poorly dressed club full of elaborately overaccessorized members, some clad all in leather. You really can't expect people to look their best when the company they keep includes characters similar to Herbert von Krolock, the ridiculous fop from *The Fearless Vampire Killers*, and those who insist on overlapping eight different kinds of necklaces.[2]

So if you see a figure stomping about shirtless, with a leather jacket hanging open over his exposed chest, chances are that's a Villainous Vampire. Their distaste for undershirts is remark-

1 See *John Carpenter's Vampires*.

2 The biggest pop culture offenders of elaborate vampire jewelry overdose include Drake from *Blade: Trinity*, Dwayne of *The Lost Boys*, Amelia from *Underworld*, Akasha in *Queen of the Damned*, and the vampire brides from *Van Helsing* (specifically Verona).

able. Although most undead and human minds would think that perhaps a jacket with long, dragging tails wouldn't be the most practical thing to purchase, it's an übervamp's go-to getup, practicality be damned. The same goes for inappropriate seasonal attire. Because vampires aren't as vulnerable to temperature changes as humans, this means they can wear whatever they want year round, See a young lady parading about in the same bushy fur coat for days in the middle of the summer heat wave, but hardly breaking a sweat? Vampire.

In a way, the media hype machine is partly to blame for these tragic vampire fashions. From the beginning, when Max Schreck's Count Orlok was transformed into the dapper but poorly styled Count Dracula on stage, famed actors Béla Lugosi, Christopher Lee, and Frank Langella continued the tired formal attire legacy with red satin–lined capes, popped collars, even plunging open shirts (thanks, Frank), topped with medallions.[3] This paved the way for sad vampire fashions among the bunch.[4] These pop culture representations of vampires with a penchant

3 Hamilton Deane, who directed the play *Dracula*, translated from Bram Stoker's work, can actually take all of the credit for bringing the overdressed caped look to vampires back in the 1920s. Deane was the first to put the count in the infamous cape, and one of his stars of the stage was none other than Béla Lugosi.

4 Dwight Renfield from *The Night Flier* actually cruises around in a full-fledged Dracula costume (cape and all) murdering unsuspecting commuters. Although his warped catlike face is frightening, the clothes are truly the scariest part of his getup.

for evil drive home the reality that Villainous Vamps appear to still be getting dressed in the dark.

So keep your guard up around those smirking shirtless lurkers who look like rejected stand-ins from a My Chemical Romance music video.

The Lackey: A Villain's Best Accessory

A great way to pick out the Big Bad is by the company they keep. Although many of the evil undead have committed to living a life of solitude, others choose to partake in the services of the sidekick. The limping, deformed manservants of yesterday are still finding ample employment caretaking for their evil masters. Granted, many Villainous Vampires have upgraded to a non-appearance-challenged helper, as it is easier to fly under the radar of humanity undetected if your escort isn't parting the sidewalks in shrieks with his overall look. Plus, no one wants a show-off.[5]

The lackey is even more useful than a harem full of vampire brides. A manservant can become a day driver, block up the windows in a mansion, even score the night's meal. In fact, lackeys have been getting organized over time. Take for example the society of familiars from the *Blade* series (each human member tattooed with the glyph of the house he serves). Not only is this clan made up of hungry followers eager to do a vampire's bidding, but the members include police officers, lawyers, psychologists, and more. It's a veritable Yellow Pages of free services, and all they need is the mere promise of immortality; they don't actually have to receive it.

---

5 See Igor; Brudah, *Count Yorga, Vampire*; and Koukol, *The Fearless Vampire Killers*.

TRICKS TO IDENTIFYING AN EVIL HENCHPERSON

- Spends the day running menial chores for a boss he fears more than death
- Is a "yes" person
- His employer's goals are his own individual goals as well (an apparent lack of personal drive or motivation)
- Has little to no personal concern for his own well-being
- Always hitting on attractive people for "a friend"
- Sometimes calls said friend "Master"
- Avoids eye contact
- Has odd eating habits (bugs, birds, worms, etc.)
- Is overly protective of his employer; does not give out names, dates, or addresses
- Will rocket into severe depression if he fails at anything
- Mysterious bruises, limps, and cuts appear from time to time; if asked about the wound's origin, it's because he "deserved it"
- Has an off-putting name or nickname
- Takes orders from a voice inside his head
- Retells "the boss's" stories with great excitement and obvious exaggeration
- Has an impressive scamper and even more effective creep
- Is often seen hauling out large and heavy black bags to the river, lake, or dump
- Lacks moral scruples
- Gives the impression that his boss is a terribly difficult and tedious and unpleasant person, yet he sees no fault in him.
- His boss is a notably powerful and extremely unpleasant person (this is true only for a henchman whose boss is an already known public figure)
- Overly protective of the trunk of his car
- Above all, exhibits unwavering loyalty

But be warned, those of you considering becoming a lapdog to the evil ones: It rarely works out in your favor. Never forget you are still rotting flesh in their eyes, as expendable as a thawed-out steak in the fridge. Justify your undead allegiance all you want—"I'd rather be a pet than cattle"[6]—you will most likely get betrayed, left behind, discovered by the authorities (or worse, your master's enemies), or devoured if it's snack time, no matter how solid your deal for fame, riches, sex, or the standard promise for eternal life was at the time. About ninety percent of all sidekicks end up as scraps between the canines of their former boss. Promises mean nothing to Villainous Vampires; remember, it was the cold boss Marlow who remarked, "The things they believe,"[7] mere moments before snapping his lackey's neck.

A RAINBOW ASSORTMENT OF TERROR:
PHYSICAL FEATURES

Skin

Similar to the other classifications, most of the physical features possessed by a vampire are used for one thing only: to serve their need to feed. Just like the rest of the vampire community, many *Hemophage sceleratus* also have alluring soft skin.

Although we may have poked a bit of fun at the Big Bad's dress code, that doesn't mean it's not a delight to watch that exposed skin dance and sway from beneath a scantily clad outfit. Granted the costume attire may make them stick out like a

---

6 Scud the techie familiar from *Blade II*.

7 *30 Days of Night*.

sore thumb in society, but that doesn't make their physique any less . . . compelling. The luscious skin conjures up all sorts of come-hither ideas in a mortal's mind. No one's complaining when they get an eyeful of the alabaster skin of a lesbian vampire queen dancing about in a negligee for your delight. It's when the half-naked lady goes to the market all done up that she causes a scene and risks unwanted attention from slayers or others that may disrupt her lifestyle. So while the overly sexed style you see a lot of vampires in does have its drawbacks, no one's exactly telling those dressed like Ingrid Pitt from *Countess Dracula* to put on a sweater. They're not about to risk covering up their greatest predatory asset.

On the flip side of their unwavering beauty, Villains can also seriously turn on the ugly. We've seen countless representations of vampires with grotesquely fair skin, creased faces, and black bags under their eyes.[8] Why is their skin so light? Many believe that an ultrasensitivity to UV rays, which keeps this variety of vampires out of the light, has caused the creature to evolve with little to no pigment in the skin. This skin affliction certainly doesn't deter them from stalking necessary prey. Again, this type of vampire dismisses the need to blend in. Some use it to their advantage; popping up with a mouth full of fang and a face like a wolf can help them shock a victim deer-in-the-headlights style.

Certain members of the *sceleratus* society have evolved beyond these two villainous skin divisions and have learned how to control their physical exterior. These creatures often swap from human form to that of a natural predator, similar to the snake

---

[8] Count Orlok, *Nosferatu*; the pasty Radu, *Subspecies*; John Stone in *A Taste of Blood* transforming into a pale skin-peeling vampire.

and the bat. It's not uncommon to find that when threatened or excited, a certain breed of vampires' epidermis will take on a scaly appearance like that of a snake or lizard—or they may just take on the form of a giant predator entirely (the bat is most common).

However, not all Villains are torn between looking frightening or seductive. The truly clever beasties can morph from one to another, unless provoked by anger or sadness. Gary Oldman's representation of this ability in *Bram Stoker's Dracula* is possibly the most notable. He went from powdered hair, wrinkled skin, and claws to long-haired, top-hatted hottie with the flip of a switch. Unfortunately for him, his emotions got the best of him when his face mutated back into that of a strange pasty cat creature streaked in bitter black tears. Truly these beings are often at the mercy of their emotions.[9]

Limbs

An easy way to identify vampires who are up to no good is by locating and analyzing the limbs of a vampire. Unique to many types of *Hemophage sceleratus* are distorted clawlike talons that have developed into hunter's tools, perfect for shredding flesh. With one swoop of his extended claw, Jerry Dandrige from *Fright Night* tore through a bouncer's neck in seconds. The claws can be used offensively, defensively, and during feedings. The nails of a

9 Pop culture has provided a fairly accurate representation of the many animal forms these creatures can mutate into. The film *Van Helsing* gives Dracula and his brides the ability to transform into giant bat beasts when angered and ready to fight; Damon of *The Vampire Diaries* can transform into a crow; there's the aforementioned snake lady stripper Santanico Pandemonium in *From Dusk Till Dawn*; and we've also seen wolves and other frightening beasts.

vampire claw are razor sharp, so remember to freeze and act with caution should you find a vampire hand creeping up your leg. Any sudden movements, jerks, or twitches could mean one less appendage.

As far as looks go, think of a twitching corpse hand, where the nails have had ample time to grow. The skin will look cracked with a yellow or green discoloration and appear stretched over pulsing veins and strangely large knuckles as if twisted over the bones. Each digit will be extended far beyond a normal length, and it seems there really is no limit as to how long a vampire digit can grow. The fingernails will be exceedingly long, cracked, and not particularly clean.

And finally, bear in mind that some breeds of evil vamps do not need to be sitting next to you in order to paw all over your precious flesh. Nosferatu hands are known for their seemingly impossible ability to reach for objects across the room. Even the shadows of their appendages can wake you from your slumber with a cold clammy shiver running through your body.

Eyes

The eyes of *Hemophage sceleratus* are rarely used in the same manner as those of other vampires. In fact, most of the eye color conversions in Villainous Vampires either happen upon turning and stay that way, or occur only when their adrenaline is raised.

The most popular eye color changes within the evil realm are the blackout (when the eye turns totally black), yellow fever (when the iris of the eye changes to a yellow hue during an adrenaline rush), and the common bloodred eye, which can indicate either an increase in adrenaline or a serious blood craving. A general rule of thumb for Villains is that any eye flash, big or small, should be taken as a warning sign. Exit the premises immediately and head toward a safe location at the first twinge of optical discoloration.

Fangs

Of all fanged beasties, the Villain has by far the most varied selection of dentition. The range and mutation of the evil vampiric incisor is a delightful collection of variety and shape for any fangophile.

The evolution of the Villainous mouth is most fascinating. Max Schreck's Nosferatu and the miniseries *Salem's Lot*'s Kurt Barlow had incisors situated right in the forefront of the mouth, making conversation impossible. Nowadays most vampire canines have crept to the sides of the jaw, making verbal communication and venturing out into the world much easier. Still, if the vampire has no need for such frivolities as friendships, then there's a good chance he's still sporting the front-of-the-mouth fang look.

Earlier, we discussed the embarrassing incident that may occur from time to time called the fang slip. Villains rarely experience this sort of occurrence, and they are hardly embarrassed by the occurrence if they do. The pearly whites are a proud part of the evil vamp's life (no matter how mangled). If they're turned on by the sight of flesh and want to spend an evening sucking on your neck or making you their puppet, so be it. If the teeth come out, the teeth come out; a *Hemophage sceleratus* will expose his canines whenever he sees fit. These particular vampires are way more about the bloodlust than getting you naked, though that doesn't mean they don't delight in the pleasures of the human flesh now and again, nor does it mean they don't commonly pick out the most handsome neck to nibble on. But it's normally a feeding-first mind-set, pleasure later (even when they're engaged in both acts at the same time).

An interesting pop culture take (possibly the most challenging to the media's perceptions of vampires) is the evolution of the fang to a more gruesome level made popular by film director and writer Guillermo del Toro. His examination of vampiric evolution has opened the world's eyes to possible futuristic mutations of the vampire species. His early work on *Blade II* demonstrated that vampires could possibly mutate further into even more vigorous hunters with chins that could snap open like a Venus Flytrap. His efforts should be applauded for continuing to remind society that this creature is not stagnant. It will continue to change and adapt and become more ferocious and capable throughout each century. Del Toro continued on with these mutated viral vampires in his work on the book series *The Strain*. The first novel truly ups the gore and shock value, introducing vampires that use stingers to inject their prey with paralyzing venom while sucking on their blood and defecating all at once, and that's not even the truly disturbing moments.[10]

HOME IS WHERE THE UNDISTURBED DIRT IS:
HABITAT

The range of personalities within this genre opens the door to a large variety of habitats. The most prevalent evil vampire habitats

---

10 Granted, we shouldn't give GDT all of the credit for keeping us on our toes for possibly frightening vampiric mutations. David Cronenberg's 1977 film *Rabid* brought us the porn star with the armpit stinger and insatiable appetite for blood. This is another excellent media example to remind us all that not all vampires come with fangs.

HAUNTS TO AVOID

Steer clear of circuses, carnivals, or boardwalks at night, specifically run-down examples. For some reason these attractions seem to draw in the undead like sharks to an open wound at sea. Don't go poking around a romantic boardwalk late at night unless you want to find the sharp and pointy end of a fang in your neck. *Buffy the Vampire Slayer* (the movie), *The Lost Boys*, *Cold Hearts*, and *Cirque du Freak* all pretty much guarantee that if you go to a carnivalesque area, you're highly likely to run into a hungry vamp or two.

Also avoid isolated, run-down motels in the middle of nowhere. Environments like this likely have zero cell reception, one phone line to cut, little to no lights surrounding the street, light foot traffic, and no neighbors within screaming distance. Motels in the rural areas are practically a bed-and-breakfast buffet for a vampire. They can murder the entire staff and the few guests, then sleep off the blood coma in a vacant room, possibly for days, before anyone gets wind of what happened. Let Jack Crow's former vampire slayer crew be an example to you all: Nothing good will come from staying in random motels.

It should go without saying, but avoid run-down houses. If there's a rumor that a place is haunted, chances are those rumors have been started for good reason: to keep you out. Make the vampires work for their meal; don't be a delivery service.

Finally, do not attend private parties where you've been invited by a mysterious lip-licking stranger when no one you know is involved. Did you get an invitation to join a club you've never heard of, promising a big feast, and yet there's no caterers or kitchen about? Get out before they bolt you in and serve you up. Check the Internet first; if there's no information about the people, place, invitation design, and so on, then there's a chance you've just been invited over as dinner for a vampire soiree. Urban legend fan sites often know the real deal, whether it seems hokey or not.

of today range from the highly secure and very expensive apartments, condos, or mansions all the way down to run-down homes in the middle of nowhere. Plenty of vampires have even been known to sleep in the dirt should there be issues on the homestead.

But overall the most important thing for *Hemophage sceleratus*'s home is that it is secure and left undisturbed. This particular vampire's constant need to feed on the living will always cause a bit of speculation to permeate through their neighborhood, so when they retreat back to their dwelling, it's important that they know it's safe. Even an abandoned building in the desert is secure if no one knows it exists.

A DISTURBINGLY TALENTED BUNCH:
UNSEEN ABILITIES

Mind Control

Vampires up to no good are usually the most skilled in the art of mind control. Chalk it up to the "if you don't use it you'll lose it" theory, but this classification has serious abilities when it comes to mind control.

Perhaps the most iconic example of the Villainous Vampire's ability to enthrall a victim is Count Dracula, demonstrated by the portrayals of Christopher Lee, Béla Lugosi, Frank Langella, and Gary Oldman (and many more). With a mere glance they can have you arching your jugular in their general direction. The count barely needed to speak a word; his powerful grasp over your mere mortal brain could have you under his spell and opening up your blouse in no time. If Superman can become transfixed by a Dracula-type beast, what chance do we humans have?[11] Also in the running for best mind seducer is the long-haired ceiling vamp from Wes Craven's *Dracula 2000*. All he needed to do was waltz by a pack of females and they were immediately rubbing their necks in anticipation.

This is the kind of thrall that turns you into either a one-note, yes-man henchmen for the boss (see the section on lackeys earlier in the chapter) or a silent and awestruck helpless victim. There's little leeway; the Villain's notorious mind control is so strong, he either stuns his victims or leaves them a little off in the head. Although you may have seen images of victims submitting to Big Bad nosferatu with wicked smiles on their faces, remember that the media tends to romanticize even the most Villainous Vampires; true, Christopher Lee often held and caressed the faces of his female victims, but remember, within moments the beautiful woman would be a lifeless heap on the floor. This particular vampire is all about the kill.

Vampire Trickery

Sometimes bad vampires like to screw with humans just for the fun of it. Vampires who trick mortals are common among the evil vamps and always end up making us meat sacks look foolish. For example, they can ruin a perfectly good meal by tricking you into thinking you're munching on maggots.[12] And if mere practical jokes aren't enough, they may even "push" your brain hard enough with their mental thrall and send you down the path to a mean bug-eating addiction. Just ask poor Renfield. Even the *Buffy*

---

11 See *The Tenth Circle, Part VI: Heartbreaker*.

12 See *The Lost Boys*.

the Vampire Slayer series featured a recurring vampire named Mister Trick who organized a little game called SlayerFest '98—a nod to the never-ending pranks humans will have to endure at the clawed hands of vampires, perhaps?

The trickery can go dark really quick as well; remember the hilarious urinal prank pulled on foolish reporter Richard Dees? Sure, witnessing a vampire in mid-blood-relief in the mirror was a jarring and funny mind job from the vampire Dwight Renfield, but minutes later Dees was playing patsy for all the vicious murders this vampire had committed.[13]

If you're strong enough in will and spirit, you can rebuff vampire tomfoolery Anita Blake–style,[14] but be warned, sometimes revealing a hidden mental talent can attract more unwanted vampiric attention (see Chapter 2, "Romantic Vampires").[15]

UP TO NO GOOD:
VILLAINOUS VAMPIRE BEHAVIOR

All Talk, No Action

Unfortunately the evil vampire suffers from the worst case of one-liner monologue syndrome we've ever heard. If you think

---

13 See *The Night Flier*.

14 The vampire hunter is well known for her resistance to mind control.

15 Vampire pranks shouldn't be confused with general vampire buffoonery such as the Joss Whedon–directed episode of *The Office*, "Business School," in which Jim convinces Dwight that he is turning into a vampire. A good vampire prank done well on a friend is always funny; persuading someone to eat a pigeon, on the other hand, is not. Mind you, if you try to prank a real vampire, you're on your own.

this sort of behavior doesn't happen in the real world, you'd be sadly mistaken. There are far too many pop culture examples to totally dismiss the idea that these vampires will stop at nothing to say something eye-roll worthy. Bad puns, cheeky prose—nothing is off-limits to a bad vampire looking for a laugh. Our personal favorite terrible vampire line of all time: "You haven't lived until you've gotten head from a vampire."[16]

WHAT TO DO IF APPROACHED

If you manage to attract a Villain's attention, you're pretty much out of luck. This type of vampire is always best handled by professional slayers. If you're unfortunate enough to fall folly to the vampire's mind control charms, foolishly neglect our advice and end up rooting around an abandoned Six Flags in the middle of the night, or just happen to be in the wrong place at the wrong time, there's very little you can do to defend yourself from the Big Bad. This would be the only case where I would suggest using the old rumor mill defense systems such as the cross, garlic, or holy water. Many vampires around have been able to evolve past these weaknesses, but you may get lucky with an old-time vampire that is still stuck in the Dark Ages and hasn't upgraded to survive in modern society.

Treat this kind of vampire attack the same way you'd deal with a street assault. Scream for help and look for a safe place. Aim for well-lit, crowded areas. You've got a higher chance of survival if you can convince a hungry vampire that you aren't worth the trouble of creating a scene.

16 See *Vampires: Los Muertos.*

WARNING SIGNS OF THE RECENTLY TURNED

- They encounter hissing cats, barking dogs, and a general dislike from animals.
- They display overly aggressive behavior.
- They exhibit a previously unseen distaste for humankind.
- Their face, eyes, hands, or skin mutates when their adrenaline is released (when you scare them, excite them, or try to fight them).
- They are often overly polite to guests: "Here, get comfortable, lie down, take your shirt off."

Take note, should you find yourself about to do battle with a Villainous Vampire, let go of any attachment you may have to the garments you're wearing because they're going to get destroyed. This species exits its unholy existence by releasing ash, pus, goo, bile, or a fountain of blood in your direction.

One final word of advice: If you're on a rescue mission to get a friend away from a nefarious vampire, chances are he's already been turned and you don't know it. He's just waiting for you to try to save him; then at the last minute he plans to bite you and screw up the rest of your life in the process. Rescue missions are a fool's dream. Vamps don't take prisoners; they feed and kill or feed and turn. Remember that when you're about to leave after a long night of fighting and your former friend bites you in the arm the second you think the coast is clear.[17]

---

17 Never forget the tragic lessons learned by the heroes in *The Fearless Vampire Killers* and *Tales from the Crypt Presents: Bordello of Blood*.

HEMOPHAGE SCELERATUS:
KNOWN SPECIMENS

Big Bad

The original sinner, this vampire is usually hundreds of years old, if not more. They have little tolerance or need for humankind, and act that way. They are cold, cruel, and unpredictable. This is not a kind to be trifled with and is best left in the hands of the professionals. Often this vampire "has a plan" for the human race, a plan that ends in our complete annihilation or total enslavement.

Known Specimens
Count Orlok, *Nosferatu*
The Master, *Buffy the Vampire Slayer*
Una, *Vampires: Los Muertos*
Lothos, *Buffy the Vampire Slayer* (movie)
Max, *The Lost Boys*
Drake, *Blade: Trinity*
Kurt Barlow, *Salem's Lot*
Akasha, *The Vampire Chronicles*
Jerry Dandrige, *Fright Night*
Kit, *The Forsaken*
Lilith, *Tales from the Crypt Presents: Bordello of Blood* ("Beautiful but Deadly" also applies here)
Jan Valek, *John Carpenter's Vampires*
Count Yorga, *Count Yorga, Vampire*
Kalika (Kali Ma), *The Last Vampire 5: Evil Thirst*
Dracula, Bram Stoker's *Dracula* (novel)
Carmilla, lesbian vampire queen, *Lesbian Vampire Killers*
Murlough, *Cirque du Freak*

Eli Damaskinos, *Blade II*
Baron Blood, *Captain America*
Dracula, *Dracula 2000*

Anger-Issues Immortals

This fierce class of vampires makes no excuses for their behavior. They think little of societal qualms or what is fair. They can be set off into a blood-filled rage at a moment's notice; often they're looking for an excuse to go off on a poor mortal.

Known Specimens

Severen, *Near Dark*
David, *The Lost Boys*
Jarko Grimwood, *Blade: Trinity*
"Evil" Ed Thompson, *Fright Night*
Razor Charlie, *From Dusk Till Dawn*
Mr. Chaney, *Masters of Horror*, "The V Word"
Cym, *The Forsaken*
Louie, *Fright Night Part II*
James, *Twilight*
Marlow, *30 Days of Night*
Angelus, *Buffy the Vampire Slayer*
Deacon Frost, *Blade*
Radu, *Subspecies*

Beautiful but Deadly

The gorgeous creatures with the big secret. They use their looks to lure in unsuspecting prey and think little about simple human emotions like love. If you're particularly unlucky they'll keep you as their lapdog for months, slowly sucking you dry until you're begging for sweet death.

Known Specimens
Drusilla, *Buffy the Vampire Slayer*
Darla, *Buffy the Vampire Slayer*
Rachel, *Vampire's Kiss*
Lucy Westenra, *Bram Stoker's Dracula*
All of Dracula's brides from Bram Stoker's *Dracula* (novel) to
     Van Helsing
Danica Talos, *Blade: Trinity*
Santiago, *Interview with the Vampire: The Vampire Chronicles*
Santanico Pandemonium, *From Dusk Till Dawn*
Countess, *Once Bitten*
Regine, *Fright Night Part II*
Victoria, *Twilight*, *New Moon*, and *Eclipse*
Diamondback, *Near Dark*
Eva, *Lesbian Vampire Killers*
Miriam Blaylock, *The Hunger*
Katrina, *Vamp*
Rose, *Rabid*

Perfectly Terrible Gentlemen
A class act, these vampires know how to entertain with the best of society. They will make sure you're at your utmost ease before striking for the jugular.

Known Specimens
Count von Krolock, *The Fearless Vampire Killers*
Béla Lugosi's Count Dracula

All-Around Undead Jerks
The classic jerk vampire. Too high up to be considered just a lackey but not important enough to have any real power. These

sad sacks are always trying to climb the next rung, which actually may give you some wiggle room for deal making. But their inept brains or snippy attitudes usually get in the way.

Known Specimens
Amilyn, *Buffy the Vampire Slayer* (movie)
Eddie Fender, *The Last Vampire 2: Black Blood*

4

TRAGIC VAMPIRES

HEMOPHAGE TRAGICUS

Poor Nicholas . . . tortured by a soul he hasn't got.

—Janette, *Forever Knight*

The existence of the tortured-soul vampire among the undead folk is a well-documented phenomenon. Humans adore the tale of the creature who has it all but is haunted by his unholy existence. Lucky for us, droves of vampires are afflicted by such a strong self-loathing psychosis and loneliness that they make up a whole classification of their own, so the tortured soul stories should never stop generating great literature and films.

These are the Tragic Vampires—those who walk alone in their own self-made darkness. This class of vampire doesn't necessarily take delight in death and continually struggles with their addiction to human blood, fighting their natural instinct to kill, and struggling to restrain their hair-trigger bloodlust. Some win, some lose, but their obsession with this internal plight against their natural urges is never far from their thoughts, giving many the exceedingly melodramatic and slightly reticent attitude that marks this class.

Although these creatures bring forth some of our most

sympathetic feelings for vampires, such feelings should in no way, shape, or form encourage you to lower your guard. There is a reason why Tragic Vampires feel and act so miserable: They've killed or want to kill at any given moment, and they're hungry, terribly hungry. The thirst haunts them all the time, though they try to survive on scraps of what their addiction requires to be satisfied. So don't get caught up in the whole "they're just not that into killing you" dogma. They do, they will, and you'll be the one stuck paying off the emergency room bills if you don't keep your wits about you.

It's important to study this somber vampire who walks the fine line between Villain and Romantic, as too many mortals have fallen under the fang trying to save a vampire who still isn't comfortable dealing with his own bloodlust.

DRAPED HEAD TO TOE IN BROODING:
PHYSICAL IDENTIFIERS

Attire

When you are seemingly carrying the weight of the world on your shoulders, accessorizing an ensemble seems a bit frivolous. This is why most of these figures stick to the rugged and easy-to-repeat look. Think a James-Dean-in-jeans-and-jacket, sexy-but-unassuming kind of look, with a few nice suits buried somewhere in the back of their closet for storage (unless they're living a metropolitan life that dictates the need to dress up daily, they will resort to a bare-basics look over and over again).[1]

---

1 Even the tragic figure Angel, who spent the better part of the final TV season in suits running Wolfram & Hart, the evil legal firm, was still continually called out for repeating the same ready-to-wear style every day. When asked by a swami (in "Guise Will Be Guise," *Angel*, Season 2) why he dressed head to toe in black

Some attention is spent on personal hygiene; after all, they're somber immortals, not savages. But overall *Hemophage tragicus* favors a streamlined, low-maintenance approach. Many Tragic Vampires live their life on the road with nothing more than the clothes on their backs, so lugging around any extra weight is frowned upon.

Also, when dealing with a serious addiction, you don't want to be attracting too much attention from humankind. Flashy getups and trinkets will inevitably draw in a flock of human admirers, and there's nothing more tempting than a group of eager-to-please mortals and their many-veined helping hands. Flying under the radar is key. A vamp will want to look good enough to get by, without arousing too much suspicion or even the smallest bit of curiosity.

SOMBER AS THEY WANNA BE:
PHYSICAL FEATURES

Skin

Besides the eternal sourpuss expression plastered across this vampire's face, another way to identify these particular creatures is by their sallow skin. Although many vampires have a practically glowing epidermis, a malnourished nosferatu can often look like a bruised, yellow, and generally unhealthy being. This is due to a diet of animals or general starvation.

It's easy to compare the Tragic Vampire to a recovering addict

---

when "it's been eighty degrees in the shade, lately," Angel responds, "I don't really have a body temperature, so . . . It's just . . . this way I don't have to worry about matching. I don't actually have a reflection, so . . . " His response demonstrates the importance of practicality over style for Tragic Vampires.

Tragic Vampires

Hemophage tragicus

because they are essentially one and the same, and they look it. Without the proper nutrients derived from human blood, a vampire will begin to look sickly and ill. Take note of these signs, and don't be so cavalier with exposed flesh around those who look exceptionally starved.[2]

Eyes

The undead eyes are another way to distinguish a Tragic Vampire from the rest. Besides the soulful look of inner turmoil and constant self-disappointment that haunts the brooding eyes of a Tragic Vampire, there are also physical telltale signs of *Hemophage tragicus*. For instance, when these vampires are malnourished, their eyes respond. They've been known to become darker, totally black, and bruised around the edges, like those of someone who hasn't slept in days. Or the whites of the eyes may turn yellow completely.[3] If you witness this ocular transition with a Tragic Vampire, think of it as a warning sign. Get out and don't come back until he's fed properly. Remind him that when he lets his melancholy affect his eating habits, he puts you and others at risk.

PARTY OF ONE:
HABITAT

Tragic Vampires can live just about anywhere. They're not particularly picky beings and can make do with whatever their

---

2 Poor vampire Eddie withered away into a pale and weak creature while Jason Stackhouse and Amy Burley kept him imprisoned in their basement as a personal V-juice on tap in the *True Blood* television series. This is an excellent physical re-creation of how an underfed vampire will appear.

3 See *Twilight, Moonlight,* and *Buffy the Vampire Slayer*.

surroundings offer up. You won't see a Tragic Vampire lounging in lavish digs; it's not conducive to brooding. In fact, many members of this class of vampire seem to prefer to wander. Some will stay in a town for a year or two, but the longer a vampire stays in one place, the harder it is to deal with the daily temptations, especially when they become his friends.

Because of this nomadic tendency, it's difficult to specify a habitat for this classification of vampire; you can find them living

HAUNTS TO AVOID WITH A TRAGIC VAMPIRE

- **Barbecues:** The smell of bloody meat flapping about in the summer air isn't a meaty hunger aphrodisiac just for humans. In general, it's best to stay clear of places with hunks of uncooked red meat, so butcher shops and meatpacking districts are completely out of the question.

- **Hospitals and doctors' offices:** Some vamps have shown better restraint than others, but it's best to play it safe.

- **Empty fields, deserts, woods:** And any other place that doesn't provide quick shelter from a possible vampiric relapse.

- **Any sort of war reenactment, including laser tag, paintball, and water gun fights:** Just the look of someone fake bleeding is enough to set off a hungry vampire. Plus plenty of the vampires of the Tragic capacity have fought in past wars; the whole endeavor could come off as insensitive.

- **Other vampire hangouts:** They choose the loner life for a reason.

- **Any place where you could foresee yourself spilling blood:** Even just a paper cut is risky, so be mindful of sharp corners, even on harmless birthday presents.

in their cars, in a condo, in an RV, or even sleeping in the ground. Should they choose to set up a permanent location, more likely than not their home will be sparsely decorated with a subtly placed painting or photo of their long-dead wife or family member (most likely murdered by their own hands in a blood craze). Decorating the walls with the innocent faces that one has massacred does wonders for the appetite, and also contributes to the eternal self-loathing emotional cycle.

That being said, should you venture out into the world with a Tragic Vampire, be mindful of inappropriate meeting places that may set him on edge. Again, we don't support cavorting with this particular species, but we're aware that sometimes it's unavoidable; San Franciscan reporters do have their deadlines—just ask Anne Rice's Daniel Molloy.

STARVING REAL TALENT:
UNSEEN ABILITIES

Tragic Vampires typically exhibit the same unseen and natural talents as the common vampires, with one major difference. The underfed vampire is a weakened being, so normally the ability to read minds, force his will upon others, or partake in any additional psychic powers will be greatly hindered. Whether it's an inability to focus or purely malnourishment from not drinking blood, Tragic Vamps are never at full capacity when they are underfed. Therefore many Tragic Vampires have either completely lost their unseen abilities, or they have extremely weakened powers.

THE MOODY BUNCH:
TRAGIC VAMP BEHAVIOR

Tragic Vampire Talk

There is no such thing as light conversation with most Tragic Vampires. You're going to be either shut out completely or subjected to long-winded sermons about a ruined life and a desperate soul on the search for redemption while dealing with "the hunger." Should you get a Tragic Vampire to talk, a difficult task in itself, make sure you've blocked off ample time to discuss years of pain, addiction, in-depth analysis of each action the immortal took postbite, the pains of his heroics, or just hours and hours of feelings banter. Whatever topic he chooses to discuss, it will be full of self-gratifying pity, moral lessons, weary explanations of how he's taken up fighting evil to save his soul, or something to that tune; whatever the topic, it will be a long conversation.[4]

Why do they launch into lengthy prose? If you manage to pry their trap open, it really all depends on the vampire. Most talk for hours at a time because they so rarely get the chance to speak (what with living in isolation and all). Others drone on because it's therapeutic to get their past dirty deeds off their undead chests.

---

4 The entire Anne Rice novel *Interview with the Vampire* is in effect a long self-loathing look into vampire Louis's miserable life (from his perspective).

But perhaps the vampire Spike has the best take on the whole monologuing self-pitying vamp. In *Angel*, "From the Dark," while Angel rebuffed gratitude from a woman he saved, Spike lent his own voiceover and opinion to the tired Tragic Vampire lecture, saying (in a mock-Angel voice), "Your tears of gratitude are enough for me. You see, I was once a badass vampire, but love—and a pesky curse—defanged me. Now I'm just a big, fluffy puppy with bad teeth . . . No, helping those in need's my job—and working up a load of sexual tension, and prancing away like a magnificent poof, is truly thanks enough! Say no more. Evil's still afoot!"

Sadly, this type of intellectual stimulation can get real old, real fast. The best advice is to stick it out and nod though the entire process. Remember: This is a moody group. A moment of disinterest can be taken as a direct insult against their tireless struggle and plight, and can incite even the calmest of vampires into a hateful bloodlust. Above all things, take their issues deadly seriously.

SUICIDE WATCH

Many vampires have a hell of a time dealing with their immortality. Combining an insatiable bloodlust with a never-ending life cycle leaves plenty of room for a lot of guilt, which is why most of the Tragic Vampires should be placed on suicide watch.

If it is your intention to keep them alive, there are two types of particularly vulnerable vampires that one should keep under close attention so they don't do anything rash: newly formed vampires and nosferatu that have lived too long and seen too much (as they may put it).

As seen in *The V Word* or *30 Days of Night*, plenty of newbie vampires would rather die than live a life as a vampire. Keep an eye on newbies as they may head straight for sunrise.

Those who have been around for centuries often engage in self-inflicted stakings. They may no longer be able to deal with how much the world has changed around them. Vampires who have lived hundreds of years tend to go off the deep end out of despair, which is labeled "the dangerous time." Many Rice vampires fall victim to this time.

One of the first Tragic Vampires, Varney throws himself into Mount Vesuvius, no longer able to live with his past actions. Even the more modern vampires today have tried to take their own lives. Moody Edward Cullen attempted to anger the Volturi into ending his eternal suffering over leaving his true love. It's hard being a vampire but letting the sunrise come and take you away is never the answer.

Real Undead Hero: Tragic Heroes

Quite a few Tragic Vamps take their guilty consciences to heart and feel the need to redeem themselves for all the suffering they and the rest of their kind have inflicted upon the human race, and subsequently, take up the hero mantle.

These Tragic Heroes use their heightened abilities for good. Perhaps they're trying to make up for the bad they unleashed on the world previously, maybe they are no longer enchanted with the evil side to their dark lives, or maybe they've risen from the grave after being sexually assaulted and murdered by a gang of predator vampires and they're just looking for some cold, undead justice.[5] Either way, there's a growing underground group of pop culture hero vampires who use their powers for good, and are good at it.

The real-life versions of these characters are exceptionally rare and prefer to remain out of the limelight. Think about it: They spend their lives destroying their own kind—beasts that the human race is not fully prepared to comprehend—and the rest of the supernatural world wishes they were ashes. Discretion and secrecy is imperative in these creatures' way of life. If they were caught in mid-vampire slay by the authorities, they would have to go to jail. And who has time to deal with the human justice system when there is a supernatural war raging on our doorstep?

Although these particular heroes harbor all the emotional issues of the Tragic Vampire, they choose to work it out on the streets. The mission to save the world from danger is more important to

---

5 See Sadie Blake, *Rise: The Blood Hunter.*

VAMPIRE DETECTIVES

If you're talking about Tragic Heroes, you can't forget the private dicks of the undead world. Although they have the same driving motivations as the stake-wielding heroes previously mentioned, these brooding vamps prefer to fight crime the legal way, or partially legal for some. Taking up jobs as private investigators and detectives, vampire gumshoes roam the streets looking for unlawful paranormal activities and solving a few human crimes along the way.

FOREVER KNIGHT

Nick Knight is trying to repay society for his sins by working in the crime-riddled city of Toronto as a detective. He's eight hundred years old and likes to use his mind control on overly pushy reporters. The series aired in Canada but started out as an '80s made-for-TV movie in America on CBS, in which Nick was played by Rick "Jessie's Girl" Springfield.

BLOOD TIES

Henry Fitzroy is a 480-year-old vampire from the television series *Blood Ties*, based on the Blood Books series by Tanya Huff. The son of Henry VIII teams up with ex-cop Vicki Nelson, who is losing her ability to see. Oh, and they totally have the hots for each other, but Nelson is in a committed relationship, which seems like canon for some of these mystery series.

MOONLIGHT

This supernatural series features Mick St. John, the vampire detective with a heart of gold. Mick is ninety years old and in love with a reporter (who is seeing someone else). Mick actually employs the help of many other vampires in solving crimes, including a tech-savvy nerd vamp named Logan Griffen.

ANGEL

Although the series ultimately turned into something more than stories of a vampire detective, show creator Joss Whedon conceived his *Buffy* spin-off series as exactly that: "a little office with the blinds and the fast patter and the sort of nihilistic toughness and the dark world and the strange turns and all of the things that you find in the great '40s and '50s noirs . . . It puts you in a world that's slightly heightened in the way that those were, so it kind of makes sense that they would be detectives."[6] Angel, who was born in 1727, opens a PI shop in Los Angeles, and from there he saves the world, many times.

them than saving their souls (though you could make the case that they're trying to buy their way into heaven). As other vampires prefer to brood and mope and isolate themselves, these immortals take action. Still, it's a lonely mission when you're fighting creatures the rest of the world has chosen to ignore. Plus they've seen the violence and would prefer to keep the casualty list low, so flying solo (or with a bare minimum Scooby Gang) is commonplace among the Tragic Heroes.

Confusing Code of Ethics: The Cavalier Vigilantes

Not all Tragic Vampires swear off the human bloodsucking. Some of them are perfectly all right with munching on the occasional human neck as long as that human is an evildoer, morals be damned. These vampires justify their need for human blood by deciding that they are, in fact, doing human society a favor by ridding it of its more undesirable characters. Red-eyed Marie from the film *Innocent Blood* fulfilled her sex and blood quota feasting on the necks of criminals.

6 Joss Whedon in an interview with GreenCine on October 29, 2007.

Does this cavalier vigilante attitude often lead to terrible mistakes? You betcha. In fact, in that same movie Marie mistakenly leaves a mob boss for dead, which in turn leads to a whole army of vampire gangsters ravaging the town. Although this situation allows for a fantastic helping of "made man" vampire puns, it's a perfect example of how vampire vigilantism is dangerous at best.

Cavalier Vigilantes are often the scourge of the Tragic Heroes' existence, as their loose regard for human life contradicts everything the Tragic Hero tries to protect. Whereas the Heroes take the plight of humankind seriously and go to great lengths to protect even the worst mortal criminals (preferring to let the justice system decide their fate), Vigilante vamps often get caught up in their own vices and undead needs.[7] And although most do try very hard to stick to a personal code of ethics, only feeding on murderers, drug dealers, and the like, the blurry line between personal justice and plain old revenge makes it likely that most Vigilante Vampires will cross it at least once in their existence.[8]

Some of these Vigilante Vamp figures are wildly entertaining jackasses whose loner statuses have left them with a personality so crass and outrageous that it would turn the polite and pasty Béla Lugosi a dark shade of red. True, many other vampires, especially the Villains, come and go and do as they please. But a Tragic

---

[7] Notorious as the most callous of the vigilante vampires is Proinsias Cassidy from the *Preacher* comics (known simply as Cassidy to his very few mates). He's cold, crass, a drug addict, and constantly dealing with the fact that he has murdered multiple people whom he cares about. This makes for fantastic conversation, and he is possibly one of the most fascinating to watch of the tortured souls.

[8] Not to mention the problems arising from simple cases of mistaken identity. Even Tragic Hero Angel misguidedly killed a demon warrior in the episode "Judgment"; as it turned out, the fallen warrior was trying to protect the very victim Angel was also trying to save.

Vampire's combination of inner dilemmas, blood addiction, and isolationism creates the perfect storm for one of the most entertaining pricks in the history of vampire classification.

You may find yourself wanting to befriend and save this type of troubled vampire whose sarcastic attitude makes them so appealing. This would be a huge mistake. The playful jerks are like that for a reason. Remember that with the Tragic Vampires, what you see is what you get. If you meet a vampire who is still dealing with addiction but charms you with his witty banter, sexual prowess, and carefree attitude toward societal qualms, he probably won't have a problem with opening up a vein right in public as well. Sure, he'll feel rotten about it for days, but you'll still be the one with half a pint of blood missing. It takes discipline and restraint not to bite into your neck, and those who make jokes still haven't fully come to terms with the seriousness of their condition. You can never let your guard down, no matter how entertaining a vampire may seem.[9]

The Romantic Hidden Beneath the Tragic

Many of the Tragic Vampires listed here have extremely high classification crossover ability. Vampires, like people, are multifaceted beings, so it's not uncommon to find a Tragic Vampire who also displays features of the Romantic classification. Often this type is miserable because they've been harboring passionate romantic feelings

---

9 Though he straddles classifications across the board, Spike is still a perfect example of those vampires who walk the line of smart-ass vigilante. When the *Buffy* vampire gets neutered (a microchip that shocks him whenever he has the intent to do harm is implanted), he's forced to release his pent-up aggression elsewhere. Cue the witty banter and nonchalant attitude toward fighting evil, for example, "I would [fight] but I'm paralyzed with not caring very much" (*Buffy*, "Triangle").

WARNING SIGNS OF A RELAPSING TRAGIC VAMPIRE

- Shaking limbs
- Exposed fangs for no apparent reason
- Rapid eye color change
- Higher-than-average irritability
- Loss of competent thought
- Imagining everything to be blood
- Unprovoked S.V.F.[10] mutations
- General lack of interest in previous passions
- Apathy toward the plight of humankind
- Missing pets
- Acts out of character (becomes strangely social)

for another. Unrequited or doomed love is often the cornerstone for morose vamps. So although a vampire may be placed in this category, know that this is not the final say on this particular nosferatu.

Take, for instance, Miriam Blaylock from *The Hunger*. This incredibly powerful seductress whispers forever to her victims and then locks them away to die a slow and painful death. Many critical eyes have gone over her seemingly harsh actions and pointed out that she does love her victims, deeply, in her own way. It is her curse that drives her to murder, and yet she still doesn't stop. Is she a misunderstood Romantic, a Villain, or just a Tragic creature doomed to live in a world where her loved ones share a few precious centuries with her and then wither away into dust? It's a difficult call, but vampires like Miriam straddle

10 Sexy Vampire Forehead (see the *Buffy the Vampire Slayer* comic, Season 8, Issue 21, "Harmonic Divergence").

the classification borders (though we think in the end she truly belongs here).

Still, the point of the matter is that Tragic Vampires are the least mentally stable out of the vampire bunch, and that's saying something. They also have the highest classification crossover potential, so you'll definitely see Tragic Vampires mentioned here and in other chapters as well.

WHAT TO DO IF APPROACHED

The lure of the Tragic Vampire is incredibly tempting because everyone loves a fixer-upper now and then. Plus their sour attitude and "I just need to be loved" puppy dog eyes make them seem like a long-lost stray just looking for the right home, which is most likely what the last foolish mortal thought before he or she woke up after a blood bender with a wrecked house, sore neck, and missing pet cat.[11] Seemingly good vampiric intentions should in no way convince you that this creature is anything more than a killer. In reality, they're underfed ticking time bombs ready to burst from hunger at the first sign of a skinned knee. There are no guarantees that if bitten in a blood rage, their vampire venom won't turn you into a vampire immediately. And there certainly aren't any promises that a vampire can make it through the rest of their immortal lives clean and blood sober. The hunger is there forever.

If approached, it's important to maintain a level head and not get sucked into the sad sob stories of this vampire's life. Stay stoic and withdrawn; show no interest, but be polite. Even the smallest

11 Think miserable old cat-eating Alex from *Tale of a Vampire*.

drop of kindness can be viewed as an invite into the safe confines of your fleshy arms, and we all know how that will end. It may also do you some good to remind the vamp that you are a family person and have people that depend on you (even if you don't)—such a comment may trigger old memories and guilt, and send the vamp reeling for the horizon in a cloud of his own self-misery.

HEMOPHAGE TRAGICUS:
KNOWN SPECIMENS

Faking It

Sadly, there are plenty of Tragic Vampires who aren't fully committed to their vegan diet. These are the types who swear they'll never drink another drop of human blood again, and then minutes later they're fang deep in someone's neck. Sure, they feel terrible about their slipup, but that's what's so tragic about this particular group: their inability to use self-control.

Known Specimens
Laurent, *Twilight* and *New Moon*
Barnabas Collins, *Dark Shadows*

Needs to Learn to Love Thyself

These vampires live a life with bouts of happiness followed by plummeting depression. They seek comfort and companionship from others but often end up murdering their loved ones or letting them die a slow and painful death. If this group could learn to come to terms with their past, love themselves, and be able to live on their own or become willing to explore fulfilling nondependent relationships, they could be much happier vamps.

Known Specimens
Varney, *Varney the Vampire: The Feast of Blood*
Louis de Pointe du Lac, *Interview with the Vampire: The Vampire Chronicles*
Proinsias Cassidy, *Preacher*
Jasper Hale, *Twilight* series
Miriam Blaylock, *The Hunger*

Conscientious Killer but Still a Murderer
This group of Tragic specimens knows that killing is wrong, and yet they do it anyway. They make no bones about trying to stop or pulling back on their needs. But they do go to meticulous lengths to make sure their victims' lives are ended in a painless way, unless you piss them off or kill their handlers.

Known Specimens
Martin, *Martin*
Eli, *Let the Right One In*
Countess Marya Zaleska, *Dracula's Daughter*

Tragic Hero
The rough-and-tumble human freedom fighters you see here are always battling for the human race, be it with science, smarts, detective work, or deadly hand-to-hand combat. They may not win all the battles, but if their hearts could beat, they'd thump for humankind.

Known Specimens
Angel, *Buffy the Vampire Slayer*
Joshua York, *Fevre Dream*
Vegan Vampire Clan, *Supernatural* (series)
Marie, *Innocent Blood*

Mina Harker, *The League of Extraordinary Gentlemen*
Saya, *Blood: The Last Vampire*
Alucard, *Hellsing*
Nick Knight, *Forever Knight*
Mick St. John, *Moonlight*
Sadie Blake, *Rise: The Blood Hunter*
Alicia, *Cold Hearts*

5

HALFIES

HEMOPHAGE DIMIDIUM

You'll be back. When the hunger knows no reason!
And then you'll need to feed, and you'll need me
to show you how.

—Miriam Blaylock, *The Hunger*

S tuck between the world of the undead and the world of the living, Halfies are unfortunate and miserable creatures going through an extended period of vampire transformation. Whether it's a full-fledged viral takeover of a human body or a suspended Vampire Interrupted phase put on hold with pills and a prayer, the process is unpleasant and often humiliating.

It is important to educate yourself on the many different signs of a person going through an undead transmutation: first and foremost for your safety, and second in order to identify and address what can (and sadly can't) be done for them.

YOU LOOK LIKE DEATH:
PHYSICAL IDENTIFIERS

Attire

Most of the Halfies seen mucking about in public are those stuck in midtransformation. Sadly, because these beings often appear more human than the rest (because they are), it's difficult to spot a Halfie by attire alone.

A few comical vampire portrayals have depicted a protagonist once bitten scuttling about, draped head to toe in all black.[1] Although the all-black garb is a cute notion, most victims waging the battle against the undead transformation appear rumpled and wrinkled. This group is now tossing and turning through sleepless nights and spending the days cowering in the shade, hardly leaving any time for laundry. Most *Hemophage dimidium* look how they feel: confused, in pain, and tired. Until they come to terms with what's going on inside them, their clothing is usually the first to suffer.

It's important to distinguish looking like a tortured hell beast and just being dirty. If you have a friend who has been showing off vampiric tendencies and all of a sudden shows up caked in dirt, pretending to be your buddy, he's no longer straddling the divide between human and vampire. He's gone through one of the many vampire siring traditions, which include being buried in the ground.[2] So if you run into a buddy who's been hanging out with the late-night crowd, and he's covered in dirt, run, because chances are he's hungry.

The Cocktail: A Halfie's Best Accessory

Halfies who have managed to exist in between life and death usually have obtained a drug that hinders the venom coursing through their veins from turning them into a full-fledged bloodsucker.

---

1 See *Once Bitten*, *My Best Friend Is a Vampire*, *Fright Night 2*, and *The Kiss of the Vampire*.

2 *Buffy the Vampire Slayer* and *True Blood* both include the act of burial as part of their vampire transformation rituals.

Halfies

Hemophage dimidium

VAMPIRE SUPPRESSANTS IN THE MEDIA (THE COCKTAIL)

PILLS—*THE FORSAKEN*

The bumbling vampire hunters from *The Forsaken* carry pills made up of antigens, aminos, and proteins that were supposedly discovered in the late 1980s during HIV drug trials by a bitten doctor. The pills slow down the weeklong turning process and can keep the virus at bay for a few years, but not forever.

PILLS—*VAMPIRES: LOS MUERTOS*

Another batch of antivampire pills was possessed by Halfie Zoe in *Vampires: Los Muertos*. Of course, once an übervamp got her hands on the meds, she took them all, gaining the ability to walk in the sunlight. This event actually teaches us all the valuable lesson to never carry around more than the needed amount of vamp suppressants (with an emergency extra).

POTION—*FEVRE DREAM*

Joshua York, a reluctant vampire, creates an alchemic potion that can control the "blood fever" inside a vampire. From the *Fevre Dream* steamboat, York sails down the mighty Mississippi looking to relieve other blood-lusting vampires.

SERUM—*BLADE*

Blade needed his magic serum concocted by old man Whistler. Rumor is it's a mix of blood and the essence of garlic. Once bitten, if injected with this juice (in its fancy gun needle) you can live on the edge between vampire and human and fight the hunger—but maintain your handy super strength to fight full-fledged bloodsuckers.

PILLS—*NIGHTLIFE, MADHOUSE,* AND *MOONSHINE*

Vampires in these books gulp down a mix of pills, including iron supplements so they can resist the urge for blood. The result is hunger suppression and a loss of some of their vampiric powers.

Any good Halfie won't be caught out of arm's length of his medication, as it's the only thing keeping him human. Meet someone who looks like hell with a pill-popping problem and a penchant for super rare steak, and there's a seven out of ten chance that you're dealing with a *Hemophage dimidium*.

TURN AND FACE THE STRANGE CHANGES:
PHYSICAL FEATURES

Skin

Those who have been bitten are in a sense dying right in front of you. Their skin generally reflects their distressed physical state, usually presenting a sallow tone, especially if they don't feed. This class shares many similarities with the Tragic Vampire because both groups tend to refrain from drinking human blood. If they don't feed they will begin to display hollow cheeks, bags under their eyes, and clammy skin.

Also important to know is that once bitten, the body will slip into defense mode and react to the venom or virus similarly to how one responds to an infection—with fever. Subjects may complain that they're burning up and sweat profusely, but their skin will be cold to the touch.

On the Inside

What's happening inside a Halfie during transformation is not a pleasant experience for friends or victim. Possibly one of the better and more gruesome examples in the media is the experience Corri goes through in *Club Vampire*. After coming home and feasting on a hamster she begins to lose her gruesome lunch and, with it, a lot of her internal organs.

What a Halfie's body is going through is the ultimate shutdown; the body is essentially withering away and becoming something new. Even if you're unlucky enough to be bitten by a vampire and find yourself pulling organs out of your body, remember that it could be worse. You could be turned by Guillermo del Toro's *Strain* beasties, in which case your privates wither up into nothing.

Eyes

The vampiric eye won't emerge in most cases until much later in the Halfie's transformation (if he is not on vampire suppressants). But if the victim is angered, scared, or placed in a situation with any sort of an adrenaline rush, there is a great chance for his eyes to change a shade or two.[3] This is usually an instance of deep shame and embarrassment for a Halfie, and it's good to minimize your shocked reaction if you witness this occurrence. Normally these transformations occur moments after an instinctual lunge toward a loved one's neck, by which time the Halfie is already feeling pretty ashamed.

Fangs

Halfie canines (if they are infected with the bloodline that mutates the jaw into a vampiric fang) do not fully develop until the victim has completed transformation. Consider the appearance of the fang the final sign of development.

What you will see on *Hemophage dimidium* are fang buds[4] or the beginnings of the nosferatu tooth. These baby teeth sit in the

---

3 See Michael from *The Lost Boys* when he's pissed and hungry.

4 In the film *Bram Stoker's Dracula*, Miss Lucy displayed a lovely set of fang buds moments before she was ravaged by Dracula in wolf form.

back of the mouth, waiting to take full shape. While in bud form the little teeth are not particularly good at piercing the skin but are still sharp.

The growing of fang buds is another uncomfortable aspect of the Halfie's plight, and you'll constantly see them tonguing away at their gums trying to soothe the two new teeth growing through their jaw. It's a continual throbbing pain, like a cavity located in the front of the jaw, and just another reason Halfies often struggle with headaches and mood swings.

SHOULD I STAY OR SHOULD I GO?
HABITAT

Halfies live one of two ways. If they have a handle on the disease, many *Hemophage dimidium* continue on with their current lives, whether it's in a high-rise condo in a big city or in their parents' basement. The other half usually hits the road looking for answers, possibly taking up with a band of slayers or hacking it out on the lonesome road alone. Rumors have it that if a Halfie kills the vampire that sired him or her, the infection or possession (depending on who you are or what bit you) can be reversed. Needless to say that puts a lot of oomph in their step. But, not everyone wants to become a hero and set out on a lonely journey across the world looking for vampires to slay. Many Halfies just want things to go back to normal; sadly, there is no lifetime guarantee on many of the scientific concoctions, and scientists aren't remotely close to a cure yet. Eventually those living with the disease will turn completely, despite their best efforts to keep living relatively normal lives.

MILD-MANNERED MIND CONTROL:
UNSEEN ABILITIES

Halfies are still growing into vampires, and even though they are stuck in the unfortunate limbo between human life and an eternity suffering from a never-ending, unquenchable bloodlust, there are some perks. For one, the Halfie will start to develop very weak mind control abilities. When used on small children and exceedingly tired and weak-willed humans, they can be slightly influential. However, complete control over these skills takes practice, full vampiric strength, and blood. Without these three things, the Halfies' powers are blurry and unreliable at best.

A JUMPY BUNCH:
HALFIE BEHAVIOR

Halfie Talk

One thing you must recognize when dealing with even a well-adjusted Halfie (one who isn't living in full-fledged denial of the disease) is that getting bitten changes everything. From now on the subject has to spend the rest of his days battling an addiction for blood along with suppressing the venom, so the whole "I'm slowly dying and there's nothing I can do about it" situation is going to be stuck in his mind like a broken record.

A Halfie will wallow in depression, waxing on a "Why me?" whine for days. You have to be supportive; because he is, in a sense, dying right in front of you, his sadness is understandable. The other reaction to straddling death is a surprising hero complex. Whether they're seeking revenge on the breed or acting as a divine instrument, a great deal of Halfies become slayers, which means you'll be subjected to long conversations about joining the ranks and fighting the good fight. You'll also be hearing a lot of antivampire hate talk.

But the common factor among all Halfies is a pervasive sense of dread; deep inside, they know what they'll end up as, and it terrifies them. This makes those struggling with the curse jumpy, judgmental, and often cruel to the ones they love. A *Hemophage dimidium* will try to keep humans at arm's length at all times and prefers to be alone most days. It's a sad thing to watch a loved one go through, but it's better than the alternative.

The Dhampir

While we're on the topic of vampire hunters, you cannot forget the strange race of half-breed vampires who were born into this world (not created): the Dhampirs. Born from one human parent and one vampire, this group has been used to hunt vampires dating all the way back to original vampire folklore in Eastern Europe.[5]

The character Blade, who was turned into a Dhampir by Hollywood,[6] is one of the more famous half-breed vampires. He

---

5 One of the earliest legends was of a Dhampir (son of Dracula) who was part-nered with a team of human vampire hunters because he could form a psychological connection to the hunted vampire and was strong enough to go against the beast in question.

6 Blade the vampire slayer was originally a man who fought the good fight against vampires in his own comic book series. He first appeared in Marvel Comics' *The Tomb of Dracula*. His only tricks, besides his dashing good looks and

retains the powers of the vampire community but has not turned into a full-fledged bloodsucker. Many Dhampirs use their vampire side–given talents to fight injustice, evil, demons, or other vampires.

The Dhampir possesses a lot of the same abilities and talents as a full vampire, such as super strength, speed, and long life (though often not immortal, most Dhampirs age extremely slowly). Most types also manage to avoid the more unpleasant aspects of the vampiric life and are able to go out into the sun and eat human food. Most important, some Dhampirs do not feel the urge to drink human blood, though this does not hold true for all types. These advantages, combined with their vigilante tendencies against their own kind, lead most full vampires to revile the Dhampir species.

Vampire or Psychotic?

If you're going to truly understand the twitchy world of Halfies, you must be aware of signs of mental imbalance as well. Not every seemingly unbalanced person is midtransformation. Like all things popular, there will always be those faking the fang, that is, pretending to be a vampire. But it's important to be able to distinguish between a faker and someone who is truly bitten, as it could mean the difference between life and death for you and them.

There are two classic and highly debated media examples of psychosis after vampire bite. The tragic story of Peter Loew in *Vampire's Kiss* demonstrates the dilemma of determining whether someone is truly turning into a vampire or faking it. Testing for

---

Afro, were a pair of green sunglasses that could block a vampire's mind control. But he was not a Dhampir. That was changed first in a Spider-Man cartoon (where Blade cameoed) and later on for his Hollywood series.

light sensitivity, fang buds, and eye flashes all help, but sometimes you have to factor in mental instability or you could end up accidentally staking a nonvampiric, deranged literary agent on the floor of his New York apartment.

Another notable and highly debated case of vampire versus nut job is George Romero's *Martin*. The fangless young boy (who claims to be over eighty years old) seems completely normal, until he sedates his victims and drinks their blood with the help of a razor blade. Romero leaves the question wide open as to whether Martin is a member of the undead or just a murderer.

If there is doubt, stay away and call the authorities. Don't be fooled into driving a wooden spike through the heart of some poor, deranged, un-undead soul, or you're probably in for a murder charge.

WHAT TO DO IF APPROACHED

Dealing with Halfies is difficult. They can easily play upon your sympathy with their tragic plight. But remember that they're still dealing with an addiction, just as a full-fledged vampire is, so treat them with the same amount of care and caution as you would any other immortal. Chances are if approached by a Halfie you're being sought after for either blood or help. However, don't be lured into a hug or close contact; your warm skin could be too big a temptation to a struggling half-vamp. Do, however, volunteer to help them check out twenty-four-hour butcher shops, darker sunglasses, and a job or school that better suits their new nocturnal schedule. Helping a Halfie find peace with his new life reduces the possibilities for a hunger-spurred attack.

HALFIE WARNING SIGNS

- Lying: If you catch a Halfie in a lie, leave, immediately. You don't know what else he is lying about.

- New and obsessive interest in your loved ones: Look for constant pawing or cuddling around the neck of family members or friends. Leave, and take your family and friends with you.

- Change in diet: Watch out if they've stopped eating their raw meat and pig blood.

- Missing pets: Theirs, yours, or the neighbors'.

- Discontinuing treatment: A Halfie who has stopped taking or is wasting a single vampire suppressant is a big no-no; the cocktail is hard to come by, so if he's giving it away, beware.

- Sudden movements: Particularly lunging at exposed skin, even if they stop themselves.

- The beginnings of an S.F.V. (see Glossary).

- A vampiric eye flash that hasn't returned back to normal after many hours.

HEMOPHAGE DIMIDIUM:
KNOWN SPECIMENS

Ticking Time Bomb

These poor saps are perfect examples of weak souls under the thrall of the vampire curse. Whether it's unending hunger or a constant longing to be with their master, these Halfies waver in and out of pain on a daily basis looking for the sweet release of the undead.

Known Specimens
Justin, *Masters of Horror*, "The V Word"
Michael, *The Lost Boys*

Caleb Colton, *Near Dark*
Star, *The Lost Boys*
Laddie, *The Lost Boys*
Mina Murray, *Bram Stoker's Dracula*
Corri, *Club Vampire*
Katrina, *John Carpenter's Vampires*
Sarah Roberts, *The Hunger*

On the Cocktail

Cranky and ready to kill, most subjects on the cocktail in Hollywood become road warriors looking for revenge while popping pills and staying in the shade.

Known Specimens

Nick, *The Forsaken*
Zoe, *Vampires: Los Muertos*
Promise Nottinger, *Nightlife*

Your Parents Suck: Dhampirs

You can't pick your family, and sadly, this crop of vampiric children was born into a half-blood world of self-hate and addiction. But they usually acquire all of their parents' best traits like super strength and speed, which they later use to kill off their family.

Known Specimens

Blade, *Blade, Blade II, Blade: Trinity*
Murat (ancient lore)
Renesmee Cullen, *Twilight* series
Nahuel, *Twilight* series
Connor, *Angel* (a class all his own, coming from two vampire
    parents but not being full vampire)

Rayne, *BloodRayne*
Grace and Connor Tempest, *Black Heart*
Alexa Charon, *Changeling*
Dimitri Belikov, *Vampire Academy*
Rosemarie Hathaway, *Vampire Academy*
Vladimir Tod, *The Chronicles of Vladimir Tod*
Saya, *Blood: The Last Vampire*
Dorina Basarab, *Midnight's Daughter*
Nothing, *Lost Souls*

6

CHILD VAMPIRES

HEMOPHAGE IUVENUS

Louis: "You see that old woman? That will never happen to you.
You will never grow old, and you will never die."

Claudia: "And it means something else too, doesn't it?
I shall never ever grow up."

—*Interview with the Vampire*

There's nothing more horrific than witnessing an actual tiny child of the night in full-face crumpled vampire mode. The smallest of the vampire kind, turned children not only are frightening bundles of terror with an appetite for blood and a look straight from the schoolyard, but out of all the vampiric kind, their existence is uneasily tolerated by both the human and vampire sides. It's the one thing we immortals and mortals all seem to agree on: a general discomfort toward *Hemophage iuvenus*.

Mortal confusion surrounding immortal youths is commonplace. For one, we take pity on those smaller than us and deemed innocent. But we know that they need our blood to survive, and who knows if that sweet little face won't open up an artery while we slumber away dreaming about our newly adopted vampire babe?

The actual act of vampiric reproduction is normally considered to occur when a human is changed to an undead beast, thus bringing him into a vampiric "family." This is why you'll some-times hear vampires refer to their makers as Mother or Father. Similarly, creator vamps may refer to their newly made vamps as children. This behavior leads to a patriarchal or matriarchal rela-tionship between the creator vamp and its offspring.

However, actually creating a vampire from a young child is considered a taboo act in vampire society and frowned on by mor-tals as well. Most vampires consider it unfair to force the life of the nightwalker on a being that may not be fully able to understand the weight of its actions. They recognize that it's problematic—and downright uncomfortable—to be trapped inside a child's body while the mind grows at a normal maturity rate.

The most infamous Child Vampire is Claudia from Anne Rice's *Vampire Chronicles*. The young girl was picked up by vam-pire Louis and turned by Lestat at the ripe age of five. But in the movie retelling of *Interview with the Vampire*, twelve-year-old Kirsten Dunst took on the role. Yes, it would have been difficult for a younger child to play such a meaty part. But perhaps, just perhaps, the mere thought of a five-year-old feasting on blood was too horrible to make her a likable character to audiences. It would seem that both vampires and humans feel that the children of the night are borderline abominations.[1]

---

1 Although both versions of *Interview with the Vampire* show that the vampire coven in Paris executes Claudia with sunlight, in the novel *The Vampire Armand*, we learn that Armand tried to give Claudia the adult body she always wanted by switching out her body with a grown woman's. His motivation? Perhaps he was willing to do anything to get her away from Louis, or just aware of the painful exis-tence of being an immortal vampire stuck in a tiny body. Still, it lends credence to the theory that other vampires are generally uncomfortable or sympathetic to an undead child and would go to great lengths to fix this unfortunate "situation."

The movie adaptation of *Interview with the Vampire* isn't the only film in which uneasy minds wrestled with the existence of Child Vampires. In the DVD commentary for *Blade*, writer David Goyer revealed that there was a scene in

MOMMY ISSUES

Perhaps one of the many reasons vampires are oh-so-uncomfortable around Child Vamps is the rampant amount of Oedipus complexes running through the vampire community. Vamps have got a thing for their moms, there's no denying it. So why would a member of the undead community want to bring another child into their confused and messed-up way of life, especially if they're already completely unhinged over their own childhood?

The proof is in the blood pudding. Anne Rice's Lestat turns his dying mother, Gabrielle, into a vampire, and after a time of happiness they eventually part, not speaking for hundreds of years. *Buffy*'s Spike turns his only friend, his mother, into a vampire who then turns on him in a fit of evil, calling him all sorts of names. In the film *The Lost Boys*, the main family is victimized by a pack of vampires all because the master wants to bring his family a new mother. Even the advertisements for the film *Dracula Has Risen* featured a creepy *Whistler's-Mother*-from-hell-type woman claiming to be Dracula's mom. There's a strange and unholy connection here that possibly explains why vampires are so averse to being parents themselves.

THAT'S ONE BAD BABY:
PHYSICAL IDENTIFIERS

Attire
Oh, the horror of a life spent shopping among the toddler or "little miss" sections of department stores. Can you imagine ripping

---

which the main woman character, Karen Jenson, discovered a jar with a vampire baby inside. Both Blade and Whistler kept the creature to run vampire experiments upon, but the studio cut this material, deeming it disturbing, as all things Child Vampire seem to be.

Child Vampires

Hemophage dimidium

through hanger after hanger of tops bedazzled with little pink bunnies, flowers, and baby chicks? It's no wonder these kids seek revenge upon the living.

There are two distinct styles of Child Vampire attire. The first are for those who embrace the unending torture that is a life trapped inside a tot's body and decide to dress the part. On the plus side, dressing like an adolescent is effective camouflage as well as a potent lure—the sight of an adorable lost child easily attracts potential unsuspecting victims—there's nothing terribly suspicious about bunnies (unless you're a vengeance demon). Children out and about at night bring out the helpful Samaritan in us all.

The second style mimics that of a preteen adult wannabe. The vamp dons adult attire in an attempt to blend in with an older crowd. This approach usually results in one of three outcomes: They stick out like a sore thumb and get unwanted legal attention; they attract possibly wanted attention from a nefarious pedophile and it ends quite gruesomely for the adult; or they're awkwardly ignored and generally avoided. Either way, should you spot a tot wandering about alone in clothes not quite appropriate for his age group, keep a distance.

FROZEN FOREVER BABY FACE:
PHYSICAL FEATURES

General

Child Vampires share the same fanged or unfanged tendencies as their makers. But most important, they seem to remain physically as young and immature as they were when they were created. They're frozen in time, or possibly growing at a grossly stunted pace.

Skin

Because of the circumstances of their creation, these children normally take on the best possible qualities of every Gerber baby. Their chubby cheeks, glimmering eyes, and flawless, baby-soft skin all remain intact for centuries. Just as older vampires often transform into the most beautiful possible version of themselves when becoming vamps, so do Child Vamps turn into the best-looking version of a child possible.

FROM CRIBS TO CRYPTS:
HABITAT

It is exceedingly difficult for vampire children to live on their own. If they're spotted out and about driving, shopping, walking, and hunting alone, it will raise suspicion, which could mean an annoying phone call to social services, followed by home visits and possible government action. Most vampirekind, be they living within a community or outside one, chose to avoid any sort of legal issue at all costs.

So what is *Hemophage iuvenus* to do? Many decide to build up family units, often by siring their own Father and Mother and building their own unholy little family. Others have found humans who don't mind taking in a vampire or two and have made a happy home leeching off their blood supply. Either way, Child Vamps should not and usually cannot live on their own. So should you meet a homeless Child Vampire, be on your highest guard. As mentioned before, it is a great taboo to create a Child Vampire; if whoever sired this creature is not around, you can go ahead and assume one of two things: one, that the vampire maker was a bloodthirsty mongrel who didn't care who or what he fed upon, or two, that the vampire who had to jump through great social hoops for his creation has now perished, by the hand of either the vampire government or their own little creation. Either way, a missing vampire family is another red flag; you don't want to be the replacement the little *Hemophage iuvenus* selects to fulfill the role of its missing family members.

Haunts

Even as Child Vampires age internally, they continue to visit the same favorite spots, including toy stores, playgrounds, late-night puppet shows, and other child-friendly arenas. For one, these are safe places where Child Vampires can feel protected and accepted. Plus child-oriented locations make easy pickings for the hunt. Not that this type of vampire has anything to worry about. Finding prey is as easy as lying down in the middle of the road. A child in distress will always draw in unsuspecting do-gooders.[2]

Other strange places where you may stumble upon Child Vampires are late-night schools. Just because the Child Vampire was sired at an early age doesn't mean he would stop going to school

---

2 This technique was actually best executed by Child Vampire Homer from *Near Dark*. He would simply throw a bike in the middle of the road, sit down, and wait. Dinner would come to him. This movie also showed the eventual dynamic that forms when you sire a child when Homer remarks, "Do you any idea what it's like to be a big man on the inside and have a small body on the outside?" And fellow vampire Severen replies, "You have any idea what it's like to hear about it every night?" The mutual resentment is almost inevitable.

all together. On the contrary, many *Hemophage iuvenus* continue their education for years and become accomplished artists, musicians, and scholars. The library isn't a terribly social place, and a Child Vampire can easily spend countless hours there under the radar. Plus, if money isn't an object, a well-paid private tutor rarely asks a lot of questions about maturity and family. Often the child is simply assumed to be an oddity or prodigy when he begins to truly excel.

SMARTER THAN THEY LOOK:
UNSEEN ABILITIES

Some of the younger vampires have also been blessed with an assortment of telekinetic goodies. They've been known to read people's thoughts and put humans in a trance; some can even project thoughts into others' minds. It's one of the small blessings behind becoming an undead child of the night. In fact, many of the vampires cursed with eternal childhood are selected by other vampires, or by fate or circumstances, because of these abilities. Becoming a vampire only strengthens and heightens their powers. Again, this is only for some, not all. Some kids just wind up in the wrong place at the wrong time.

BRATS AT ALL AGES:
CHILD VAMPIRE BEHAVIOR

Vampire children are unnerving, creepy specimens who can turn their malevolent charm on you at a moment's notice. Even the world outside the undead-obsessed knows this. They are an accident waiting to happen. While their bodies remain frozen at whatever age they were turned, their minds continue to mature. But no matter how many years tick by they will forever be looked upon as children, even by their so-called peers. This is enough to make Child Vampires storm clouds of unpredictable anger. Don't engage a Child Vamp in an argument or attempt to cheer up a gloomier than average *iuvenus*; you'll most likely end up with fang marks all over your legs.

WHAT TO DO IF APPROACHED

Getting out of a skirmish with a Child Vampire is a difficult situation. There are so many negatives stacked against you. For one, what if you're wrong and your pint-sized opponent is mortal? Congratulations; you've just beaten up a child and you're going to jail. But even if you're correct, if you're spotted by an ignorant Good Samaritan passing by, you risk being interrupted, giving the Child Vamp the perfect opportunity to escape or gain the upper hand. The best thing to do when coming into contact with a tiny vampire is to stay far away at all times.

The Child Vampires' biggest issues are their stunted height and limbs. They need to find a way to draw you into attack range. This can all easily be attained by tricking their prey into helping them carry things, assisting them from a fall, or even comforting them—who can resist a little lost child with tear-filled eyes and beautiful skin? The second you're within arm's length, you'll be locked in their steel jaws.

WARNING SIGNS OF A CHILD VAMPIRE

- The child speaks in complete sentences with proper grammar.
- He often corrects you on your terrible grammar.
- Sometimes you hear the vampire in question use retired phrases such as "Golly!" or "Gee whiz!"
- He knows entirely too much about history for his apparent age.
- In turn, the subject doesn't think you know anything about history and is often lecturing you about the past as if he witnessed it himself.
- The child sometimes drinks hard liquor.
- He is incredibly skilled at a number of hobbies that would take mortals years to master.
- You find yourself shocked that this infant appears to be a great deal more mature and smarter than yourself.
- He "accidentally" talks about the past like he was there first-hand, and then covers it up.
- The youth doesn't know where the local schools are.
- The subject has no friends his own age.
- He doesn't possess a book bag or any school supplies and is tragically unaware of text talk or any other sort of child slang.
- The kid wears clothes way too expensive for his family or lifestyle.
- The child laughs scornfully at you when you attempt age-appropriate communication.

HEMOPHAGE IUVENUS:
KNOWN SPECIMENS

Wild Child

An unfortunate side effect to turning a Child Vampire is his general lack of willpower combined with his smaller stature. Inject an adult-sized dose of vampire DNA into a child's body paired with a lack of self-control, and you've created a single-minded eating machine. He'll kill whatever is in his path for food; sustenance and self-satisfaction are the most important goals in his life.

Known Specimens
Lenny, *The Hamiltons*
Danny Glick, *Salem's Lot*
Little Girl Vampire, *30 Days of Night*

Young in Face, Old in Mind

A slightly less volatile group than the "Wild Child." These vampires have ancient knowledge hidden behind their cherub cheeks and tiny smiles and often possess massive inferiority complexes as well. They've lived for years, some for centuries, and in that time the little buggers have become aces at manipulation and murder. Some are good, some are bad, but all of them are smarter than they look and rightly inspire fear.

Special attention should be paid to certain members of this society. Often Child Vampires are created as part of a spiritual rite that can elevate them to almost evil godlike status. Some young vampires are actually super evil reincarnations of ancient baddies, and for some reason the unholy powers find it particularly clever to have the exterior be that of unassuming youth. The cleverest Child Vampires survive for centuries thanks to the pity they can inspire in other vampires and humans alike, and they can often amass great power as they get older, rising to the upper echelons of vampire society. At this point, they must also invest in powerful bodyguards to avoid a potential mutiny.

Known Specimens

Claudia, *The Vampire Chronicles*

Eli, *Let the Right One In*

Divia, *Forever Knight*

Homer, *Near Dark*

The Anointed One (Collin), *Buffy the Vampire Slayer*

Charlotte, *Blade: The Series*

Sweet Little Things

These creatures are few and far between. This kind of Child Vampire actually acts like a child and lives a virtually stress-free existence. They don't kill, and they don't hurt others. This group is as close to a real child as you're going to get for vampires. But sadly they're not easily stomached by hardened bloodsuckers and vice versa. They're usually represented in the media in cartoons, sitcoms, and Disney movies. They are not harmless, as they still possess two canines twitching for blood.

Known Specimens

Gabrielle, *Charby the Vampirate*

Shori, *Fledgling*

Rudolph Sackville-Bagg, *The Little Vampire*

Just a Kid

Sadly, in the world of baby vampires, some poor creatures never turn fully and live their in-between stages as someone's assistant or lackey. Although they still struggle with cravings and seem torn between two worlds, they are still very much little kids and will age (very slowly) until they give in to their carnal desires for blood. But more on Halfies in Chapter 5.

Known Specimens
Laddie, *The Lost Boys*
Darren Shan, *The Saga of Darren Shan*

7

VAMPIRE TRIBES, CLANS, COVENS, AND CLUTCHES

HEMOPHAGE TRIBUARIUS

Come on, be one of us.

—David, *The Lost Boys*

The undead path can be a lonely one. Although many vampires choose a solitary life, there are plenty who take solace with other members of their kind. But as with the many personalities of the nosferatu, the social hierarchy of a vampire clan is important to be educated about, to ensure that you always stay one step ahead of the black shadow of the vampire.

NOMADS

The first gaggle of vampires and possibly the most violent are the Nomads. This type of troupe travels from town to town raising unholy hell in their wake. They care little about who they pick off for dinner and don't bother with playing it low-key in person. The vast sprawl of empty countrysides and small-town "keep to yourself" attitudes keep this bunch relatively safe; plus they rarely stay in the same place for very long anyway.[1] That said, when it comes to vampire extermination they are usually the first to be attacked, because eventually their bold and brazen lifestyle leaves a trail for slayers. Moving from place to place doesn't allow this gang to build up much of a resistance or defensive strategy, because all they have are the clothes on their backs and they are generally trying to evade rather than engage. Although they're left pretty vulnerable, danger is still the way of this pack. Make it a rule of thumb to stay clear of any unruly and new faces that appear in the middle of the night in a lonely one-horse town.

HOUSEHOLD HAREMS

Some vampires mimic the Dracula way and keep a small but familial group nearby at all times. Now, the vampire definition of family doesn't necessarily mean the *Interview with the Vampire* way of life that plays out like *My Two Unholy Dads*. The more common familial vampire representation is made up of one head-of-the-household vampire and their small but loving harem of brides and/or grooms.[2] The harem's job is first and foremost to fulfill the wishes and demands of the master; next to looking effortlessly sexy at all times, they spend the rest of the day pleasing the master (of course) or any houseguests who need entertaining. The supernatural world of the nosferatu is by far the most

---

1 *John Carpenter's Vampires, The Forsaken,* and *Vampires: Los Muertos* are all good examples of vamps taking residence in run-down towns in order to keep a low profile.

2 Vampire harems run rampant through pop culture, including *Van Helsing, Dracula: Dead and Loving It, Bram Stoker's Dracula, The Vampire Lovers,* and *Lesbian Vampire Killers.*

Tribes, Clans, Covens, and Clutches

Hemophage tribuarius

open and welcoming of all sexual preferences. In fact, vampire pop culture has been pushing the bill on sexual equality issues long before it was popular for werewolves and other paranormal beings to get involved in Hollywood.[3]

The patriarch of the group is usually the head of the household and the one who decides who lives and who dies and becomes a member of the household harem. He has the final and solemn say in just about everything the harem does, from excessive chanting (*Dracula: Dead and Loving It*) to whether the family is going to begin breeding tiny hell babies (*Van Helsing*).

SOPHISTICATED CIRCLES

Higher up the ladder of vampire social hierarchy are the elite organizations: vampires who come from money or have wisely invested and now can live in a veritable commune with their own set of rules and regulations. Often this group's business constitutes a large part of the human economy, and they own and operate large corporations.[4] This group of vampires lives with the best of everything: clothes, homes, tools, and more. But living with these corporate-minded vampires means constant assimilation talks, plotting, and strategizing—often with little action outside the boardroom.[5]

---

3 *Carmilla*, the groundbreaking novella published in 1872, featured lesbian vampire characters and is still looked at as a sexually revolutionary text.

4 A few famous examples are Ziodex Industries (synthetic blood refinery, *Underworld*), the Denham Corporation (*The Satanic Rites of Dracula*), Berm-Tech Industries (telephone company, *Netherbeast Incorporated*) and Russell Winters Enterprises (*Angel*).

5 See the vampire series *Blue Bloods*, *Underworld*, *The Vampire Chronicles*, and *Twilight*'s Cullen family.

VAMPIRE ELITE

The governing system of vampires includes the elders, ancients, highest of the high, and respected lawmakers and punishers of vampirekind. Most elders live separately with their peons and assistants and come together only in a time of great emergency. Still, they are the highest and most powerful among the vampire society and live in the lap of luxury and knowledge.

Depending on the bloodline, every vampire societal governing system is different. For example, in the *Blade* series the vampires are governed by an elite group of ancient purebloods (those born into vampirism). The class of vampire beneath them (never to have a seat at the elders' table) are those who were sired into the vampire plane of existence, or bitten. With the number of purebloods depleting by the century, it's no wonder there was a revolution.

Many vampire governments are run similar to the *Blade* scenario. The oldest look out for the youngest, because they have experience and know-how. Of course, some societies are more open for "bitten" vampires to take part in executive decisions; Anne Rice's vampires have a fairly good system of checks and balances. Just because you're an elder vampire (Akasha) doesn't mean you have all the answers and can dictate the relationship between humans and vampires across the globe.

But no matter how the system is run, in most cases it's regulated by a group of elders, while the business at home is usually taken care of by the head of the household.

THE HIERARCHY OF A VAMPIRE CLAN

In order to further understand the idiosyncrasies inside the personal world of a vampire, we've broken down the structural makeup of a vampire group commonly found in nomadic tribes and small gangs.

Leader

The head of any vampire gang usually tends to play fast and loose with both danger and power. This combination makes the head of the coven sometimes unpredictable, callous, or cruel, but always charismatic. He's fought his way to the top, so he's got to possess a certain amount of charm even if it only appeals to the undead. Still, it's not all blood feasts and bats at the top. There will no doubt be at least two to three members within the coven gunning for his position. This makes treachery common, and the leader is often additionally cruel and somewhat paranoid as he anticipates betrayal from every corner. But perks abound: The leader is the first vampire to receive the spoils and glory—both material and mortal—of any endeavors, often choosing the prime human victims for himself. Although being the leader does affix a giant bull's-eye on his back, the survival rate isn't terribly low. Even after exceptionally brutal beatings and assassination attempts, he often somehow finds a way back to the top (though the process is usually very painful).

SURVIVAL PROBABILITY: 7/10

EXAMPLES: David, *The Lost Boys*; Kit, *The Forsaken*; Marlow, *30 Days of Night* (charming in a vampire way we humans wouldn't understand)

Second in Command

The leader's most trusted advisor and "number two" is burdened with the day-to-day operations of the vampire coven. But this does not mean he's the leader's lackey; quite the contrary. In order to excel as the leader's potential successor, the lieutenant vampire needs to have a firm grasp of logic. He often must be the voice of reason when tensions are high. It's true that the number two often ends up on the business end of many of the leader's emotional outbursts, but he usually gets his own back by schtupping the boss's lover or even secretly planning a full-fledged mutiny with the rest of the ranks. But if his double-dealing is discovered, he is guaranteed a swift and painful dismissal from his position—and his existence.

SURVIVAL PROBABILITY: 8/10

EXAMPLE: Kraven, *Underworld*; Amilyn, *Buffy the Vampire Slayer*

Comedic Outlet

Wanna get promoted out of the lower ranks of a coven? Find a sense of humor. Just becoming slightly more interesting than the muscle or a lowly foot soldier will improve your survival chances. Granted, you may have to pick up an annoying catchphrase or be prepared to laugh hysterically at even your superiors' worst jokes, but at least you'll only be called upon for menial jobs that involve cracking a one-liner and maybe a few human heads. It also doesn't hurt for Comedic Outlets to scar themselves or dress slightly different from the rest of the group, as this allows them to stand out even more. Sadly, Comedic Outlets have a lower survival rate purely because they do tend to stick out. Still, it's a higher position in the coven than the jock members and doesn't require much thought, just the capacity to be obnoxious.

SURVIVAL PROBABILITY: 6/10

EXAMPLES: Pen, *The Forsaken*; Santiago, *The Vampire Chronicles*

Eye Candy

An important part of any coven is the Eye Candy. The best-looking member of the group can fulfill one of two roles: pretty worthless or pretty deadly. Both are fun, but the "pretty worthless" Eye Candy has a slightly better chance of survival because he most likely won't be participating in fights. "Pretty deadly" is the coven's secret weapon: They kill and they're hot, so they'll throw an attacker off guard. The other is there predominantly to fulfill their role as nothing more than Eye Candy. Both examples must look good in all situations and environments; after all, it's their job to make sure the group is keeping up with appearances. Think Star in *The Lost Boys*: She didn't really do much other than tell everyone what they already knew, but you could watch her say it for hours. Eye Candy may or may not have affairs with the number two, but their other job, aside from looking good, is keeping the boss happy. If you ever run into a pack of vampires, the Eye Candy with seemingly no real skills is your best chance for an ally if you have nothing else to barter with (unless you can appeal to number two, who's usually always gunning for a hostile takeover of the group).

SURVIVAL PROBABILITY: 6/10

EXAMPLES: Star, *The Lost Boys*; Mae, *Near Dark*; Harmony, *Buffy the Vampire Slayer* (TV series); Cym, *The Forsaken*; Santanico Pandemonium, *From Dusk Till Dawn*; the many incarnations of Dracula's brides

Troubled Outsider

What group would be complete without the self-loathing sulky member who wavers back and forth between murdering his compatriots during the day or turning the stake on himself? Often the Troubled Outsider is a recently turned vampire or a Halfie still struggling with the transition from human to vampire. Expect this character to mope about daily, dragging his feet and continually complaining about the facts of vampiric life. This ne'er-do-well often ends up initiating the entire group's demise by either trying to get himself out of his vampire predicament or selling out the group for leverage somewhere else.

SURVIVAL PROBABILITY: 8/10
EXAMPLES: Caleb Colton, *Near Dark*; Michael, *The Lost Boys*

The Brain

Every group needs a smarty-pants chemist, scientist, or learned person (or at least someone to strut around pretending to know the facts). This member shouldn't be allowed to make large group decisions, but if you need to build a better werewolf bullet or add some spice to the synthetic blood, he's your undead man. Brains generally stay out of the fray and can often survive a bloodbath because they don't usually get involved in physical altercations.

SURVIVAL PROBABILITY: 8/10
EXAMPLES: Logan Griffen, *Moonlight*

The Muscle

Vampire Muscle is a funny subgroup within a clan. Vampire "grunts" don't necessarily have to be big and bold to be brutal enforcers. In fact, some of the most intimidating pop culture Muscle vamps rely only on their deeply troubled psyches to scare and intimidate humans. Who needs linebacker shoulders when you're not afraid to open up someone's throat in front of the entire room? Sadly, those who go charging headfirst into the climactic fight have crappy survival rates, but more often than not they exit in a blaze of glory.

> **SURVIVAL PROBABILITY:** 5/10
> **EXAMPLES:** Reinhardt, *Blade II*; Jarko Grimwood, *Blade: Trinity*

Foot Soldier

These faceless drones do the bidding for the rest of the group. If you realize that no one knows a thing about you in your coven, let alone your name, chances are you're a Foot Soldier and one red shirt away from dying on a vampire away mission.

> **SURVIVAL PROBABILITY:** 1/10
> **EXAMPLES:** We can't be expected to remember the names of these hapless characters, can we? They're merely fang food, after all.

8

LIVING IN AN UNDEAD WORLD

REAL-LIFE APPLICATIONS

I have never met a vampire personally, but I don't know
what might happen tomorrow.

—Béla Lugosi

N ow that you've been briefed on the many different classifications of the vampire race, it's time to put all of that knowledge into action. It's only a matter of time until you'll find yourself face to fang with an immortal member; it's a small undead world after all.

The following is a breakdown of a few commonplace occurrences and the appropriate responses that should help you get a handle on the whole "assimilating your world with the living-impaired" thing.

HOW TO APPROACH SOMEONE WITH A DEATH WISH:
THE VAMPIRE INTERVENTION

No matter how many bodies pile up, there will always be some unfortunate person in your life who doesn't completely understand the implications of joining up with Team Vampire. Too many people fall prey to the way the media campaign portrays the vampire life as a "sleep all day, party all night" lifestyle.

Should a loved one become enchanted by the children of the night, the best way to reach her is by hosting a detailed and thorough Vampire Intervention. This is not an act to be taken lightly. It takes planning, patience, and a great deal of effort. By following these steps, hopefully your loved one will be swayed away from the bloodsucking way.

Get Educated

First and foremost, if you're going to approach a person who is on the path toward vampirism, you must become knowledgeable of the facts. Find out and study everything you can on the type of vampire the subject is obsessing over. Make yourself aware of the subject's motives.

- Is he wrapped up in an undead relationship and under the assumption that turning himself will bring the love to a new pinnacle?

- Has she been consorting with a Big Bad fanger, jonesing for a chance to join up with his unruly gang?

- Has one of his loved ones recently been turned?

- Is this being considered an easy out, because of unfortunate life circumstances?

- What type of bloodline is she looking to hitch her veins up to?

You must have informed answers for all of these types of questions so you can properly address the threat to the subject's mortality. For instance, if the subject has fallen under the love spell of a Romantic Vampire, you will need to approach the situation from a different angle. Why is he seeking out love from dangerous places? You may want to involve a relationship therapist and inform her of the subject's past emotional struggles.

If your loved one is hungry to feast on the blood of a Big Bad type of Villain, she may be under the thrall of a nosferatu. Then it's not just an intervention that you'll need to be planning, but also a full-fledged spell-breaking session that snaps the connection between victim and host.

Should the person in question be gunning for the life of the immortal because a loved one has been turned, the person's grief is understandable. You have a few options based on the type of vampire the former loved one has become. If he's transformed into a mindless killing machine, perhaps you should hire a vampire expert to document his current attitude and changes to share with the grief-stricken lover. And if you can control the situation and circumstances, a monitored field trip to the damned's new place may be in order. Although it may be heartbreaking to witness someone coming face to face with the soulless shell of his former familiar companion, watching that loved one lap up a quart of blood should aid in turning the bereaved's opinions. If, however, the subject is looking to join his turned loved one in an immortal unlife together, physically removing him from the vicinity and intervening directly with the turned companion may be in order; all but the most soulless of vampires prefer to avoid subjecting those closest to them from the same fate, even if it means they will lose them forever. (Unless the vampire involved is a Romantic Vampire, in which case he will put up a token resistance but typically succumb to his mortal mate's wishes, particularly if the mortal mate's life is at stake, which it often is.)

It's also important to assess the bloodline of the vampire the victim is enticed by; getting turned by an ancient vampire, although very rare, would give the victim unlimited abilities (versus being turned by a diluted half-breed vampire). This is important to know, as you'll have to build your case more carefully, sharing the cons of becoming linked to such an ancient line (such as being unable to go outside during the daytime).

Round Up the Troops

You'll need to assemble a support group of professionals and caring parties for the individual undergoing the intervention. Gather friends, family members, respected coworkers, and those who may be been nibbled on in practice by the vamp hopeful.

Seek the Help of a Professional

It is imperative to have a vampiric interventionist on hand for the meeting. Seek the help of someone who specializes in occult obsessions, specifically dealing with the nosferatu. This professional will be a reasonable voice amid the chaos and screams of "You tried to eat my dog!" managing to steer the intervention and keep the room calm.

Do not, I repeat, *do not* use a slayer to host the intervention. Although slayers may be knowledgeable about the subject matter, their number one response to matters of this magnitude is stake first, ask questions later. It will be more beneficial for everyone to have a neutral, levelheaded, and informed member of vampiric lore to offer up options as opposed to bloody action.

Put It to Paper

Be direct; think of this as the last time you'll ever be able to talk to this person while she's still mortal, as it very well may be if the intervention doesn't work. Put yourself in this state of mind so you're able to speak from the heart.

Use constructive feeling words. Do not attack; instead of using "you" statements, share your wishes as "I" statements. Stay away from accusatory hurtful exclamations. Statements such as "You're a terrible bite junkie charmed by the undead" will only cause the subject to go on the defensive, and nothing will be accomplished if the intervention turns into a screaming match. Keep calm, speak from your heart, and do not attack or blame; for example, "When you hang out all night with vampires I feel fear. I am frightened when you hiss at me. I'm worried you will get imprisoned on an assault charge the next time you bite someone's neck."

Compile a List of Helpful Alternative Options

Keep a list handy of possible alternatives to this lifestyle. So she wants to join a vampire in unholy matrimony? Gently remind her that there are other options besides turning; for example, some human/vamp relationships have actually worked long-term. If it's a desire to team up with a group of rabble-rouser vamps, offer up other alternatives and outlets for her aggression.

Is he searching for fame? Suggest that he start a band. This approach can also offer camaraderie. (I apologize to the family members in advance for the inevitable Billy Idol–meets–Lestat groups that will no doubt be born out of this suggestion, but at least they will be safe and mortal.)

Is she looking for danger? Tell her to switch occupations to something physical that incites and demands adrenaline control: join the armed forces, work in construction—is the *Deadliest Catch* gang hiring? Still not enough danger for her? Time to pick up a hobby. Extreme sports are always a healthy option.

Is he in need of a little anger release? Set him up with a trainer, perhaps someone who can teach him them how to spar, box, and get all that angry tension out. Then once you're convinced the aggression has subsided a little, see if he's open to team sports.

Is she feeling alone? Offer up heavy volunteer work. There she'll be surrounded by people in need of real love and attention, which will hopefully pull her focus off her own misery and remind her that there are bigger problems than her own.

Is he sick of the sunlight? Time to take up night jobs.

The most important thing you can do is harness your own aggression, speak from the heart, and *listen*. Troubled souls are often attracted to the vampiric way. Find out what the underlying psychological issue is, and work from there. If all else fails, you can throw her into a psych ward to buy you some additional time, as many doctors today still don't recognize vampires as a real threat.

EIGHT STEPS TO A SAFE VAMPIRE RELATIONSHIP

Alas, even though we've warned against it, and in spite of the fact that most vampire and human relationships end in bloody tears, there will still be plenty of you who decide to pursue a romantic relationship with a vampire.

So in hopes of imparting some wisdom to those who leave common sense behind in the name of undead love, here are some helpful steps to keep you, hopefully, bite free. But no promises.

1. Determine Whether It's Love, Lust, or Possession

Come to grips with your emotions before you dedicate the rest of your mortal life to an immortal relationship. It's no secret that Romantic Vampires are well versed in the art of seduction. It's their undead gift, but you need to suss out whether what you're feeling is the real deal or merely the aftereffects of a fang-gasm. Ask yourself:

- Do you dream about the vampire only in purely sexual scenarios?

- Do you think about your intended night and day and often find yourself daydreaming about different ways you can better perform his bidding?

- Have you experienced loss of time around him for hours or even days?

- Have you ever found yourself inexplicably running errands or feeling compelled to donate your blood, specifically to his private stash?

- Do you sometimes hear his voice in your head asking you to do things you normally wouldn't do?

- Do you complete those commanded mind-controlled tasks?

- Do the two of you only go on dates inside his crypt (apartment or manor)?

- Does he only want to see you when he's overindulged on blood?

- Is your undead adored angered by talk of an immortal future together?

- Have you been kept in the dark about your loved one's past life and kept at bay from his associates?

- Have you ever been scared (in a bad way) for your safety around your undead mate?

REPEAT RELATIONSHIPS

Catch your vampire calling you by the wrong name? Or have they ever brought up a past event you shared that you don't remember, or couldn't have possibly been alive to witness? Time to do your research. There's a good chance that your beloved isn't dating *you*, but rather the shell of their former love.

It's creepily commonplace for vampires to repeat relationships if you just so happen to be the reincarnated body of their long-lost love. These repeat offenders normally keep dusty old portraits or a locket hidden somewhere in their abode. If you find an image of a person who looks just like you at the old-timey photo booth, you're being repeated.

The film *Fright Night* has a particularly gruesome oil painting of character Amy that illustrates this point beautifully. But take solace in the fact that you're in good company. Prince Mamuwalde from *Blacula* lost his Luva in 1780 but found Tina, who he believed to be her reincarnation in the 1970s. Granted she got turned into a vampire and they both died, but there could have been some fun times in between all the stalkings. Other repeat relationships include Francis Ford Coppola's adaptation of Bram Stoker's *Dracula*, which added an entire love affair between Drac and Mina Murray, whom he believed to be his reincarnated wife Elisabeta. The brothers in *The Vampire Diaries* fight over Elena mainly because she looks like their old vampire flame (and maker) Katherine. Steamy vampire Alex from *Tale of a Vampire* moons over Ann who reminds him (and another immortal stalker) of his long-lost Virginia. Even the adorable George Hamilton version of Count Dracula is victim to repeat dating when he woos a NYC model who reminds him of his first love.

If this particular problem is happening to you, address the issue head-on. Find out if they're dating you merely for your physical similarities to their long-gone lover. Be prepared for the worst, because nine out of ten times, the answer will be yes. If so, it's probably best to terminate the relationship before they sire you in fear of losing their first love all over again.

If you answered "yes" to two or more of these questions, you're most likely partaking in an unhealthy vampire relationship, or dating a vampire jerk, or even worse, a Villain (especially if you're losing time and hearing his voice in your head). You should strongly consider alternative options for dating (werewolves are uncommonly loyal). If you answered "no" to all of the questions, make sure to keep these scenarios in the back of your mind as possible warning signs that you're on a dangerous path. But take some comfort in the fact that you may have found one of the rare "good egg" vampire anomalies. Hopefully your relationship will make it through the cravings, mood swings, and outdoor issues (but never forget that you're dealing with a blood addict).

2. Know What's on the Menu

This should really go without saying, but do not date a non-vegan vamp. If you feel comfortable sharing your life with someone who has no qualms about murder, then maybe you shouldn't be in a relationship after all. In fact, you shouldn't really be out and about in the world. You put your own life and everyone around you at risk when you condone this type of behavior. Just saying.

Although plenty of vampires don't need to kill to feed, that still doesn't mean they're safe. Think of it this way: You wouldn't keep a pet in the house that sometimes bites hard enough to draw blood (whether or not you believe it can restrain itself). Despite what you think, this isn't just about you and your safety; it's best to stick to the vampires who refuse to drink from an actual person. Synthetic blood, blood banks, and animal blood are all fine substitutes for the real thing, no matter how much the partaker complains. (Certain exemptions can be made for sexual encounters, depending on the type of vampire and your own willingness to allow them a little nibble; see the section on setting boundaries later in this chapter.)

Even with the vegan vampires, you're taking great liberties with your own life as well as the lives of those around you. Everyone makes mistakes, but you certainly don't want to expose your family, friends, and pets to the possibility of getting drained.

3. Guess Who's Coming to Dinner?

Another point of caution you should take under consideration while dating a vampire isn't just your beloved's diet, but his friends' needs as well. It's almost inevitable that your vampire love will put you in the presence of other vampires; this can be both a positive and dangerously negative situation as well.

Whether your darling is a stand-up member of the undead club or not, your paths will invariably cross with both good and bad vampires. Be it a Saturday night gang of buddies ready to throw back a warm A-positive beverage, or a past foe out to settle a score from the Civil War, you will have to deal with other vampire dietary issues and attitudes.

Not all vampires are human-friendly, and when dating a vampire you will meet both humans and vamps who will look down on your union. You need to be prepared for both sets of prejudices.

Set the rules early; for example, no vampires who kill should ever be invited into your abode, poker night or not. Also do not attempt to win over your lover's buddies on your own; make sure that if you're in the presence of other members of the immortal world, your significant other is always present. Don't be afraid to ask him to consider letting old ties to bad vampires go. But approach this request in a mature and calm manner to avoid a

DEALING WITH THE EX

It's inevitable your vampire is going to have an Ex. But, unlike most relationships, the vampire emotional baggage regarding past loves is a lot heavier on the soul. Chances are, their Ex is dead or undead. If they've passed on, consider yourself lucky because the latter is even more difficult to deal with.

Got a new lover with a long-gone mortal family? Deal with it as you would deal with any sensitive subject with a human. However, if they murdered their Ex in a fit of rage or bloodlust, you'll be dealing with a lot more residual guilt. First, make sure they've learned how to keep their rage issues in check—you don't want to be next on the list of whoopsies. Second, talk about it. Don't let it sit in the closet decaying like your lover's last meal. Bring it out into the open and deal with the grief together, then move on.

Should you be dating a vampire with Ex vampire lovers, good luck. Here are a few safety rules: Never pick a fight with their Ex; he or she will murder you in a second. Never sign on for a bonding boys' night or ladies' night with an Ex, no matter how much your lover may consider it to be fun for you. Remember, they may have left their Ex to wean themselves away from bad habits, like eating humans, so watch yourself. Finally, think how someone who will live forever might feel if their forever love left them for what was commonly considered a snack? Most likely, the vampire Ex is planning a fatal "accident" for you.

fight: "I'm afraid so-and-so wants to eat me" is a pretty direct way to handle it. If he puts up a fuss, then perhaps this isn't the vampire for you.

As far as humans who are anti–vampire love, be wary as well. You're breaking new ground should you choose to take your love public, and you need to be ready for possibly rude questions from other mortals. The best way to get around uncomfortable situations is to introduce your undead friend to those who are confused, and let them make their minds up for themselves. Be patient, but do not tolerate vampiric slander or violence. You may find that you too may also have to give up a few members of your friend circle if they go off into the deep end of aggressive and abusive vampire hate.

4. Set Boundaries

Before you hop into the coffin with a member of the vampiric race, make sure you lay out the ground rules. Setting appropriate and mutually respected boundaries could save your mortal life.

Just as you would with any mate, make sure the vamp knows the deal-breaker moves during intimate moments. In the heat of the moment, when the lights go down and the fangs come out, make sure you and your undead partner are both aware of what is acceptable behavior. Setting the rules ahead of time avoids uncomfortable and possibly lethal "accidents."

For instance, if you're planning on incorporating a little nibbling in the bedroom, know the level of lethal vampire venom your significant other holds in his system. Some kinds of vampires only need to break the skin and the slightest bit of venom will begin the turning process. If this is the case for your vampire, fang play should be off limits unless you use a retainer-like fang guard. Think of it as a vampire prophylactic.[1]

---

1 Not to be confused with the actual vampire condom, which is an all-black latex condom being sold on the Internet. It's packaged in matchbooks, and its motto is "Vampires Always Get Invited Inside."

5. Become Vampire Correct

Certain attitudes and actions in your life will need to be tweaked a bit if you want your vampiric love relationship to last. Learn the difference between slanderous vampire slang and cute pop culture terms. Check out the glossary in the back as a reference guide. Also, rid yourself of silver jewelry and gratuitous religious symbols. Although the Mark of Cain vampires are rare these days, they still exist, and they're not particularly fond of religious paraphernalia. This doesn't mean you can't continue with your religious practice; you just need to be mindful of actions that could potentially harm your mate. This particular type of vampire is most vulnerable to these ancient traditions, so it's best you remove from your home objects that physically cause pain to your vampire. Sit down with your vamp and talk openly about offensive or dangerous items you may be holding in your house; decide together what should be kept and what should be removed. Remember, you wouldn't leave offensive material on display in your home for a human guest; a respected vampire should be treated the same. Get educated on what *is* and *isn't* offensive, and keep it in mind as it applies to your daily routine.[2]

The pop culture TV series *True Blood* (based on the Sookie Stackhouse book series) isn't far off with its Hollywood representations of the high tension that exists between vampire rights groups

---

2 Household items that could cause pain or discomfort for your vampire are as common as table salt. Ancient supernatural lore has hailed salt as a deterrent for the undead. The theory is that if you sprinkle seeds or salt on the ground, a vampire will have to stop and count each grain before he can cross over. Now imagine if you spilled a shaker on the floor of the kitchen. That's a lot of time spent sorting grains if you're not around to stop him. Another sore spot for vampires is roses and other thorned branches. Boughs of these types of pricklies have been cited in folklore as the only means of restraining a member of the undead.

and antivampire activist groups. Both the Fellowship of the Sun (antivampire) and the American Vampire League (provampire) are interesting examples of some of the many underground organizations out there in the real world. Granted, the vampire's supernatural struggle isn't playing out on the television for the world to see, but it's still as intense and heated a debate as ever.

Know the hot-button issues for your vampire mate, be they tension within his own echelon of government or the neighborhood watch. He will appreciate the effort you put in, and the time and care you invest in this area will allow the two of you to function as a couple without other issues getting in the way.

6. Be Explicitly Honest

Never forget that you are dating someone with immense powers and the ability to take action against mere mortals, including you, with a flick of a pale wrist. A vampire in love is a dangerous thing if you are not clear and concise with all of your intentions and interactions.

For example, imagine the guilt you'll feel when you wake up to discover that your old junior high bully has been mysteriously dropped from the top of a tall building, but not before losing copious amounts of blood. Why is your old bully deceased? Because the night before, you got tipsy with your vampire beloved and drunkenly shared how mean and nasty the bully was to you back in the day, before admitting that you'd like nothing more than to see him served a plate of cold justice. A vampire, someone who has wavering respect for the fragile mortal condition, could easily take that as a sign or hint. Even if he doesn't think you implied murder, he could consider it an act of passion: the ultimate gift.

In order to prevent murderous misunderstandings, it's imperative that you be completely clear with your intentions, even when spoken in jest. Make sure to make it known that when you say things to the tune of "I wish he could be dangled off the Empire State Building by his ankles," your vampire doesn't run off to go surprise the unsuspecting subject of your ire.

7. Give and Take

If you're dating a vamp, you're going to have to give up some of your sunny days in trade for a healthy relationship. Sure, you could attempt to keep your vampire partner awake in the day and out of the harsh and skin-charring sunlight (if he happens to be a non-sun-friendly type). But forcing a nocturnal species to live in the day is both cruel and unusual. In fact, it could even be dangerous for *you*, as prolonged daytime exposure can be directly related to a vampire's moods and behavior. The longer you keep a vamp awake, the hungrier he's going to get. And you don't want a vampire snapping at you.

Sacrifices must be made in order to keep both sides happy. Rotate nights versus days, and make sure you both get out of the house on some nights. Just because it's dark doesn't mean you can't enjoy the night. Try looking for late-night spots as a surprise for your undead other. It will show him that you're not completely dependent on him to carry the evening part of this relationship.

Also it's important to be receptive to experiences that may normally seem strange or foreign to a human. You probably never had a fang-gasm before either, but wasn't that worth the risk of trying something new? Be open to new experiences that are safe with your vampire.

Something needs to be said about respecting each other's space as well. As you get to know one another there will be a lot of uncomfortable moments you'll both need to work through.

HIGH SCHOOL VAMPIRES

It's impossible to discuss pop culture vampires and not discuss the sudden influx of vampires attending high school. Now that the stigma surrounding vampires and sunlight has been revealed to be false for plenty of bloodlines, it's allowed some vampires to live a more "normal" existence.

Still one has to be suspect of the motivations of all these ancient and aged minds desiring to repeat basic algebra. Most vampires we read about popping up in high schools are hundreds of years old. What's the real appeal there?

And how do you reconcile the general creepiness of the vampire's actual age next to the sixteen-year-olds they're in class with and falling in love with? (Edward, Stefan, we're looking at you guys.) At least the TV series *Vampire High* separated the vampires from the mortals in their own private underground boarding school. Still many pop-lit vampires are flooding the high schools, from *Vamped* and *Blue Bloods* to *High School Bites*. Institutions like the House of Night from *Marked*, where marked young vampires are sent to learn about their new powers or die, seem a bit more realistic. And yet these hundred-year-old vampires can't seem to get enough of the public education system.

Still, there are vampires that get sent to high school that age. The lamia vamps from L. J. Smith's Night World novels can get older just like humans. This particular bloodline of vampires is born into vampirism. They grow and age but have the ability to stop the aging process whenever they see fit, which is a nice trick for them. But if a lamia has stopped the aging process and then later decides he would like to start it up again, he will age rapidly to his real physical age. Another vampire similar to the lamias is the half-human vampires from *My Best Friend Is a Vampire*, who age (if bitten but not killed and brought back to life), but at an incredibly slow pace compared to the rest of the world.

Until then, if your vamp's eyes go completely black, his forehead rumples, veins pop up on his cheeks, or you witness any other type of vampire adrenaline reaction, make sure to give your vamp the space he needs to feed in private.

8. Never Drop Your Guard

Even if the two of you pinky-swore over a coffin to love and cherish each other all the immortal days of your life, there's no getting around the fact that you're hitched up to something that feeds on humans. Make no mistake: Things can go wrong, and you could end up on the business end of a fang.

You may consider it a sign of weakness in your relationship, but you should be prepared to defend yourself against even your most dearly loved vampire friends at all times. It's the safest thing for you and those around you. Like it or not, precautionary steps are an important part of securing your happiness. If you are educated and prepared for a possible vampiric slipup, you'll know what to do in the event your lover takes a toothy dive at your little sister. Imagine if you weren't prepared: You could be out a sister *and* a lover.

Keep a makeshift vampire kit in your bedside table or somewhere else nearby. Yes, you will probably catch hell if he discovers it, but just say your jerk uncle gave it to you and you haven't had a chance to throw it away yet. The contents should simply be anything that will repel a raging hunger attack. Consider holy water, a cross, garlic, wolfsbane, or a bit of salt—having a variety of contents on hand helps increase the odds that at least one will work against your vamp.[3]

3 You don't even need to make your own vampire kit; the market is practically teeming with travel-size Nosferatu insurance. The kit itself isn't a new idea; in fact, an 1800s vampire kit was sold for $14,850 at an estate sale in Natchez, Mississippi,

VAMPIRE SELF-DEFENSE 101

In a worst-case scenario it's important to know just how to defend yourself against the fang. We've already covered specific deflection tactics for various vampire classifications. But here is a list of general need-to-know defense tactics. Though we've said it before, we feel we should say it again: These are to be used as defense only; leave the assault and offensive moves to the professionals.

Your Most Vulnerable Areas

Get familiar with all of the most vulnerable points on your body. It should be no surprise that these are all major arteries and veins. Take note of these areas, and do your best to keep them protected from prying canines.

The Jugular

This vein runs down along the side of your neck. If this throbbing artery is pierced, you're in big trouble. The jugular connects directly to the heart and maintains a strong flow of blood between that muscular organ and the brain. It's the superhighway to your blood, and few people can even stand up straight if their jugular has been tapped, let alone ward off an attack, so keep it protected.

---

in October 2008. It contained candles, a cross, holy water, a Bible, a gun with silver bullets, stakes, mirrors, and garlic. It's one of many vampire kits circulating in the world today. (Many have wound up in museums. One in particular sits at the Mercer Museum in Doylestown, Pennsylvania.)

The Ulnar Artery

The ulnar artery is a commonly accessed point of entry for both vampire friend and foe. Whenever you see a vampire bite into his own skin to share his blood, it's from this artery in the wrist. This attack is often done under the guise of friendship. So be careful when offering your hand to a nosferatu; you're only a few digits away from a problem artery.

The Median Cubital Vein

The median cubital vein is the big blue line running down the inner side of your arm. Although not as dangerous an attack point as opening up the jugular, it's still a problem if a vampire gets his fangs in there.

The Great Saphenous Vein

This is perhaps the most scandalous of weaknesses, as it's located in the inner thigh of the victim. A professed favorite of many vampires, as it is perfectly positioned on the highest part of the inner thigh, it's a veritable keg tap to a human's circulatory system. But in order to allow a vampire to get there . . . well, we don't need to tell you that. This particular vein should be looked after during romantic affairs, be they of the "one night" variety or more long-term.

Defense Moves

Although it would be great to tell you that everyone should keep a trunk of crossbows, hatchets, and stakes in their living room, Buffy Summers–style, the reality is we cannot condone unauthorized use of weapons. There's no such thing as a close call when a human has been accidentally impaled by a wooden stake. Our advice: Leave the big guns to the trained slayers and Dhampirs.

But you should know a few easy moves to help get you out of a vampire entanglement.

Yell First

You've got a better chance of escape when approached by a vampire if you yell for help. Not scream, yell. Think of all the times you've heard someone scream and wrote it off as people fooling around; that person could have been eaten by a vampire, and you wouldn't have even known. Yell clearly and loudly, "Help!" or "Fire!"—anything that will draw quick attention to you, as vampires hate a crowd and a sticky situation. Chances are he'll let you go and try to pick off a quieter snack. Don't yell out "Vampire!" because you'll most likely receive laughter instead of aid. The rest of the world is in the dark.

Hit Them with Your Best Shot

Although we strongly suggest yelling first, should you need to go on the offense, we suggest hitting them where it hurts. Vampire genitalia (in almost all cases, minus a few Guillermo del Toro beasties) will respond to both positive and negative touch. Whack 'em dead center where it counts and bolt. Don't stick around to watch what happens. The next best spots for a strike are the eyes, nose, and throat, but as a vampire's body no longer functions like that of a human, the chance of real damage is slim.

Run Like Hell

Run toward a crowded, well-lit area. This doesn't mean a creepy boulevard; shoot for popular venues, like a Starbucks packed to the brim with people. Remember that a commotion can be used in your favor to scare off an undead attacker.

WHAT TO DO IN THE EVENT OF A VAMPIRE UPRISING

Although the probability of all the vampire kinds uniting is slim (vampires are notoriously solitary folk unless in a gang [see Chapter 7]), the occasional vampire uprising has been happening since the ancient days. Even today, you can see clippings of small vampire skirmishes where bold undead minds have tried to take over a community center or even a town.[4] As long as there are evil vampires, there will always be plans to overthrow humankind. However, the world-domination ambitions of evil vamps are usually kept in check by professional hunters and, more often than not, their own kind.

Vampires know that the world needs humankind, but that it's about maintaining a balance. As of right now, vampires lack the technology to wipe out the human race completely, so thankfully, as long as they continue to need our blood, we're safe, in a manner of speaking. Plus, what are the fangers stuck in the night supposed to do during the day? You need someone around to take care of this planet in the light.

But if a vampire revolution were to take place, you should hope you've been kind to the nosferatu who respect the balance of nature. Because you're going to need them to protect you from hell on Earth.

Consider an all-out vampire revolution akin to a nuclear

---

4 If you're a loyal newspaper reader, it's likely you'll occasionally read a suspicious article in which a group of "ruffians" has tried to take over a location, yet is mysteriously thwarted from causing any more trouble by sunup. And every once in a while, you'll get something really special like the *Boston Globe*'s report of a vampire teen uprising in the Boston Latin Public School on March 26, 2009.

crisis. There isn't a safe place to turn, so it's best to lie low in a sealed-from-the-inside bunker and wait it out. Honestly, you're no match for a vampire army, and if you're around if the good vamps lose, you should be so lucky as to be used as mere food.

The best idea is to gather as many supplies as possible, find a bomb shelter, and close it in around you. And for goodness' sake, check everyone's pulse before closing the door.

GLOSSARY

A full list of vampire slang, lingo, and ancient terms so you'll be able to translate even the oldest language of vampirekind.

autovampirism The act of drinking one's own blood; this act will not, however, sustain a hungry vampire.

awakening The first time a vampire comes to grips with his new senses, abilities, and vampire state. It usually happens moments after the vampire has been turned completely and is conscious.

Big Bad A commonly used term from Joss Whedon's *Buffy the Vampire Slayer* signifying an evil being, particularly a higher-up evil being who presents a great threat to humanity. The master would be considered a Big Bad, but not one of his many minions.

blood bond The act of ingesting a vampire's blood and letting him drink yours as well. This builds a bond between vampire and human, often allowing the vamp to know what you're feeling or thinking at any given time. It's very intense and should be created only with a trusted vampire, because you'll be giving him a complete pass to your thoughts. The blood bond is commonly referenced in the Southern Vampire Mysteries but is prevalent throughout vampire media.

blood play The sexual act of drawing blood for pleasure; it can be considered a fetish among humans, but for vampires it's just getting a little hot and heavy.

the cocktail A collection of pills, shots, or serums that keep a Halfie's vampire virus in check. It will not cure the vampire virus but can keep it under control.

day driver A human or supernatural creature that can walk in the day and chauffeur its vampire master around. Must own car.

Dhampir A half-vampire/half-human who was born into his state, not bitten. The Dhampirs have been around for years, and Gypsy lore has them as some of the first vampire slayers. This trend continues in popular vampire culture today. Another commonly used term is *Dunpeal*. Inappropriate and slanderous labels of this kind are *Half-Breed* and *Half-Blood*.

donor A willing and walking blood bank for vampires. A human kept around "just in case" the vampires need her veins. A donor can also be saved if she has truly unique blood and tasting it is more of an act of pleasure and enjoyment, like a wine tasting, rather than a feeding. Virginal blood is rumored to be one of the finest blood vintages, and some vampires believe it restores their youth. This term also has a negative meaning in some vampire circles and can be used sarcastically for those forced to give up their own blood.

elder An ancient and influential member of a vampire bloodline. Usually a controlling member of that bloodline's government who has the final say on vampire debates and disputes.

fangbanger A person who is sexually promiscuous with vampires; not a kind term.

fang-gasm The act of reaching full sexual stimulation with a vampire. This term is also used for people who reach full sexual stimulation from a vampire bite.

fangophile Someone who is obsessed with the vampire culture, people, heritage, and species as a whole.

fang slip The often inadvertent act of fang presentation when a vampire is sexually stimulated, excited, angry, or hungry.

fledgling A term used by a sire or maker for his vampire children.

glamour The vampire ability to alter a human's memory. This phrase was more commonly used in Wiccan practice, but the Southern Vampire Mysteries series has claimed it for vampires now as well.

goons A slanderous term for vampires, originating in *John Carpenter's Vampires*.

maker A vampire who has created another vampire will take on this title. Some bloodlines have limited power over those they have sired. There is an inherited level of respect and position given to the maker from his "children," though it's up to the kids if they follow this social vampire etiquette. Sometimes also called *Master*, *Mother*, *Father*, or *Creator*.

nest A habitat where more than one vampire lives.

Nudger Created in the *Twilight* series, unborn Dhampirs are now starting to be referred to as "Nudger," the nickname Bella gave her child in the final book by Stephenie Meyer.

sanguine An ancient term for *vampire* or *blood drinker*.

sire Another label for a vampire who turns a mortal into a vampire. It can also be used as a verb: *sired* or *siring*.

S.V.F. Sexy Vampire Forehead, a nickname created by Joss Whedon's Harmony Kendall, the high school student from Sunnydale turned vampire, turned secretary, turned reality TV star in Joss Whedon's *Buffy the Vampire Slayer* comic series. In Season 8, Issue 21, "Harmonic Divergence," Harm finally gives a title to the rumpled forehead Whedon's vampires have been sporting for years whenever they are feeling the bloodlust. Granted, the "editors" of Harmony's new reality TV series in the comic were guessing that this was what she was implying.

turning The actual act of transforming from human to vampire. A fully formed vampire who has undergone his awakening can also be referred to as *turned*.

vegan A vampire who does not feast on live human blood. There's a fairly large debate over whether vampires who drink harvested blood (not forcibly taken but donated) should be considered vegan vampires. Right now the lines are blurred, but a vegan vampire is normally a vampire who doesn't drink human blood at all. Instead they feed on animals.

venom The serum in vampires' saliva, teeth, or blood that allows them to transform humans into vampires once it's introduced into a human's circulatory system.

the virus Whatever element the vampire bloodline contains that changes humans into immortals. It can be mutated T cells, red blood cells, or an actual virus that attacks the human body—the term is a general one.

Whedonesque/Whedonverse Used to describe something from the mind of Joss Whedon, creator of *Buffy the Vampire Slayer*.

RESOURCES

Ashley, Leonard, RN. *The Complete Book of Vampires*. New York:
Barricade Books, 1998.

Barber, Paul. *Vampires, Burial and Death: Folklore and Reality*.
New York: Yale University Press, 1988.

Karg, Barb, Arjean Spaite, and Rick Sutherland. *The Everything
Vampire Book*. Avon, MA: Adams Media, 2009.

Melton, J. Gordon. *The Vampire Book: The Encyclopedia of the Undead*.
Canton, MI: Visible Ink Press, 1999.

Ramsland, Katherine. *The Science of Vampires*. New York: Berkley
Boulevard, 2002.

Stevenson, Jay. *The Complete Idiot's Guide to Vampires*. New York:
Alpha Books, 2009.

ACKNOWLEDGMENTS

This book is dedicated to the family and friends who dealt with my strange occult obsessions as a child. Thanks for never hesitating to purchase the latest set of plastic fangs. To my editors, Meg Leder and Jeanettte Shaw: Thank you for your faith and support. To the pop culture vampires who changed the world: Béla Lugosi, Barnabas Collins, Spike, even that shiny Edward fellow. And finally, to all the people who pause when walking by a dark corner, linger just a second longer past a cemetery, and daydream about a vampire enrolling in your school: May you safely encounter a vampire all your own.

INDEX

Page numbers in *italic* represent illustrations.

ABOUT THE AUTHOR

Meredith Woerner's obsession with the fanged masses started at an early age. While other kids donned the princess getup for Halloween, she opted for the vampire bat cape, pointy ears, and dark circles under her eyes. From there she grew up always looking in the shadows for a vampire friend, begging her human pals to start a band of misfit cowboys and go *Near Dark* style. And then she met Buffy. The combination of pop culture and the undead changed the way she viewed vampires forevermore, thanks to the clever scribblings and directorial eye of the great Joss Whedon. From then on, she knew it was time to meet a member of the long and fangy club. Meredith continued her search for vampires by pulling nightshifts as a city desk copy assistant at the *New York Post*, where she learned what they really meant by "the city that never sleeps." During her time at the hub of all things sensational, *Us Weekly*, she traveled the country meeting the tastemakers of today while secretly trying to plant seeds for a *Lost Boys* second coming. Combining her supernatural know-how with a pulp pop awareness, she now writes daily about all the things that go bump in the night at Gawker's sci-fi blog, io9.com. She continues to catalog all things vampire and was there when the teeming masses lifted their voices to the sky at the first San Diego Comic Con *Twilight* panel, and she knew the next wave of fang had arrived.